Gender Dilemmas
in
Social Work

Issues Affecting Women in the Profession

edited by
Patricia Taylor
Catherine Daly

Canadian Scholars' Press Inc.   Toronto   1995

Gender Dilemmas in Social Work:
Issues Affecting Women in the Profession

First published in 1995 by
Canadian Scholars' Press Inc.
180 Bloor St. W., Ste. 402,
Toronto, Ontario   M5S 2V6

Canadian Cataloguing in Publication Data

Main entry under title:

Gender dilemmas in social work: issues affecting
        women in the profession

Includes bibliographical references.

ISBN   1-55130-044-3

1. Sex discrimination in employment – Canada.
2. Women social workers – Canada. 3. Sex role in
the work environment – Canada. I. Taylor, P.A.
(Patricia A.), 1936–   . II. Daly, Catherine, 1941–   .

HD6060.5.C3C35   1995   331.4'133'0971 C95–931982–1

Page layout and cover design by Brad Horning

Printed and bound in Canada

Dedication

The editors would like to dedicate this text to their families particularly Moe, Adam, Andrew and Jeremy, who supported our efforts with enthusiasm.

Acknowledgements

To our colleagues whose knowledge, talent and efforts fill this text with fresh ideas and understanding about the role of Canadian women in social work, we offer our thanks and respect.

To the students of social work who, hopefully, will learn from our collective wisdom, we anticipate that the theories and ideas included in this text challenge your present thinking, stimulate new thinking and shape a dynamic approach to the gender issues inherent in social work that will have a positive impact on the future direction of the profession.

Our appreciation is extended also to Ann Merner who typed and retyped the edited manuscript with endless patience and a supportive sense of humour.

Patricia Taylor and Catherine Daly

About the Authors

Leslie Bella, B.A., M.S.W., Ph.D., has taught in social work at Memorial University, St. John's, Newfoundland since 1989. In addition to a variety of papers on professionalization, her work includes an evaluation of Alberta's Family and Community Services program, a political history of Canada's National Parks (*Parks for Profit*, 1987) and an analysis of women's work in creating family through reproducing ritual (*The Christmas Imperative*, 1992).

Emily Carasco, LL.B., LL.M., S.J.D., has taught at the University of Windsor Faculty of Law since 1980. She has written and taught on issues related to women and the law and has a book forthcoming on Canadian youth and the law. She has served as chair of the Equity Employment Committee of O.C.U.F.A., editor of the *Canadian Journal of Women and the Law*, and was recently elected president of O.C.U.F.A.

Katherine Chan, B.A., B.S.W., has been actively involved in women's issues in Windsor. She has a wealth of experience in working with marginalized groups and is currently pursuing a career working with adolescent girls and young adults.

Kathleen Dilworth, B.A., B.S.W., M.S.W., was the recipient of the University of Windsor Board of Governor's Gold Medal for highest academic achievement when she graduated from social work and is particularly interested in women and stress.

Pamela Milne, B.A., M.A., Ph.D., is an Associate Professor of Religious Studies at the University of Windsor, where she has taught since 1972. She has published extensively on a range of topics in her speciality, including feminism and religion. She has been active as the chair of the University of Windsor's Status of Women Committee, member of the Review Committee on Employment Equity and chair of the Ontario Confederation of University Faculty Associations Status of Women. Pamela was named "Windsor Woman of the Year" in 1990.

Joan Pennell, B.A., M.S.W. Ph.D., is an Associate Professor of Social Work at Memorial University where she has taught since 1991. She is presently the co-principal investigator for a project on the "Family Group Decision Making Process" and is in the process of writing a book on research as empowerment. Joan's research interests and numerous published writings focus to a large extent on various aspects of women's studies.

Darlene Simpson, B.A., B.S.W., has an academic and professional background in creative writing. She has worked in the publishing industry for several years and is currently functioning as a freelance editor, writer and independent feminist researcher.

About the Editors

Patricia A. Taylor is a Full Professor at the School of Social Work, University of Windsor where she has taught courses in "Women's Issues," "Health Care," and "Practice" since 1968. In addition to being the first female full professor and first female elected director of the Windsor School, Professor Taylor has served on the executive of many local social work boards as well as the Ontario Hospital Association, Social Work Section, the Ontario Family Service Association, and is currently Vice Chairperson of the board of Family Service America, Inc. Professor Taylor is co-editor of two recent texts, *Social Work Practice in Health Care* and *Social Work Administrative Practice in Health Care Settings*, both published by Canadian Scholars' Press. Professor Taylor has also published extensively in both Canadian and American Journals. In the fall of 1994, her chapter on "Health Care in Canada: Under Stress," appeared in the 1994 edition of *Canadian Social Welfare* by Francis and Joanne Turner

Catherine Daly, B.A., M.S.W., M.P.H., Ph.D., has taught at York University, Ryerson Polytechnic University and the University of Hawaii. She is presently an Associate Professor at the School of Social Work, University of Windsor, where she has taught since 1989. Her research and publishing has been entirely focused on women's issues. She is presently conducting research on professional women and their attitudes towards feminism.

Table of Contents

Introduction

Patricia Taylor
Catherine Daly

The multi-dimensional factors that define power in our society have had a devastating impact on women in general and women in social work in particular. Problems with professional status and social acceptability plague women in social work in a unique way. One of the main themes of the following textbook explores the effects of the systemic social inequality that has historically described women as "the weaker sex" and the impact that this inequality has had on the profession of social work. In fact, the dualistic thinking that underlines the Canadian gender debate is critical in social work because of the preponderance of women in the profession. To date the social work response to this quandary has either overemphasized or ignored the gender issue. The worker, as such, is typically depicted as "nurturing" but sexually "neutral." This textbook aims to move the student beyond gender neutrality to what Mary Catherine Bateson describes as "... the need to make the invisible visible" (p. 5). Social work students must understand that while women's experiences and background may be different from men they do not speak in a "different voice," more caring and nurturing than men (Tavris, 1992, p. 85). Equality demands that the wisdom of women must be acknowledged. Indeed, in the profession of social work, the insights and creativity of female social workers are critical to developing strategies that will promote equality and improve the status of the profession as well. Consequently, students are encouraged to reflect on the diverse perspectives represented by the authors in this textbook as well as the provocative issues that they address in order to better understand themselves as both social work practitioners and social work promoters. Lack of power is the root of inequality. Self discovery will lead to empowerment (Bateson, 1990, p. 5). Exploring the historical, religious, medical, social, legal, occupational and global contexts of women's lives will enhance our comprehension of gender and equality. This work, in turn, will change the profession of social work and the women in it.

Assumptions based on gender stereotyping have always constituted an impediment to women's status in social work. As Mackie (1991) stated, "the belief that women and men possess different qualities and abilities, and should thus undertake different activities ... has often adversely affected women in social work" (p. 92). In the first chapter of *Gender Dilemmas in Social Work*, Catherine

Daly explores the impact of historically based ideas about women and their relevance to the current status of women in social work. In a similar vein Darlene Simpson suggests that science has always been used to justify women's biological inferiority. In fact, the historical heirarchial structure of health care disempowers women and has an adverse effect on women as both consumers and providers. Religion has also enforced inferiority and conformity among women. In her chapter, Pamela Milne explores the way that religions have limited diversity by describing the gendered features of religions and how, with few exceptions, women have been controlled and excluded from significant religious roles. Patricia Taylor examines how sex role stereotyping confirms the belief that men are assertive, dominant and powerful and women are nurturing, emotional and dependent. This type-casting limits women's ability to handle power and authority in the profession. Similarly, beliefs about women have integrated at various times to constrain women's equality in Canada. Emily Carasco explores, in detail, how the law has promoted gender inequality. In the area of women abuse Joan Pennell calls on social workers to question conventional beliefs about women and families. She stresses the importance of listening to women's stories, so that social workers can reappraise how they respond to violence. Without such knowledge social workers "remain ignorant of [abused women's] experience, of the effect of the response or the lack of response to the violence they experience."

In exploring recent strategies of occupational closure in social work, Leslie Bella notes that these result in either social work subordination to another profession or in the de-skilling of the profession. She concludes: "The professionalization of social work poses a dilemma for women through offering increased status, it can also have the potential to enhance conflict and completion between women and other professionals." As a result, registration initiatives by various social work associations have had an ambivalent effect on women's status. In chapter eight Catherine Daly analyzed equality in social work from two theoretical perspectives on feminism, i.e., enhanced authority and equal rights. Inequality is manifested on a continuum ranging from codification in law to covert social pressure. The former is written in legal statutes that constrain women's political and personal rights. The latter is contained in values and beliefs about women and their role in society. Ideological barriers to women's equality are often both subtle and pervasive. Kathleen Dilworth and Katherine Chan suggest that curriculum changes in schools of social work that reflect the needs of women, will frequently encounter ideological resistance from faculty, field personnel and students. However, the authors emphasize that reluctance to recognize women's needs in the curriculum will limit female student's self-esteem and independence. This textbook concludes with a final chapter by Patricia Taylor and Catherine Daly in which multidimensional factors of women's status and their impact on social work education are analyzed from a global perspective.

All of the authors have approached their topic from a feminist perspective. Consequently, several themes (such as equality, empowerment and gender) recur throughout the book. Placing women's experiences at the centre of these discussions challenges most theoretical frameworks in social work and other disciplines. The challenge for women in social work is to question the unequal distribution of power and equality in the profession.

The editors acknowledge a bias in this textbook as all of the contributors are either female professors or recent female graduates of schools of social work. At the same time we view this limitation as an advantage. As members of a privileged group of educated women we have experienced the inequalities, analyzed their meanings and are committed to change not only in the educational realm but in the community at large. This book is basically optimistic about the potential for social and economic equality, particularly in social work. Our sincere hope is that students will be excited by *Gender Dilemmas in Social Work* and will advocate social justice for women in the profession and in society.

References

Bateson, M.C. 1990. *Composing a Life*. New York: Penguin Group.

Mackie, M. 1991. *Gender Relations in Canada: Further Explorations*. Toronto: Butterworths.

McLaren, A.T. (ed.). 1988. "Creating a Canadian Women's Sociology." *Gender and Society*. Toronto: Copp Clark Pitman.

Tavris, C. 1992. *Mismeasure of Women*. New York: Touchstone Books.

Chapter I
An Historical Perspective on Women's Role in Social Work in Canada

Catherine Daly

During the nineteenth century in Canada, a widely held system of beliefs existed about women, their character and their role in society. These beliefs were destined to influence future ideas about women in social work and to shape the directions they followed in their efforts to gain professional status as social workers (Baines, Evans and Neysmith, 1993).

This system of beliefs has been referred to as the "proper sphere," the "cult of true womanhood," the "cult of domesticity," "women's sphere" and as the "love and/or duty ethos of the female world" (Cook and Mitchinson, 1976; Cott, 1977; Bernard, 1981; Welter, 1966; Prentice, Bourne, Brandt, Light, Mitchinson and Black, 1988; Gannon and Gill, 1987).

Five major ideas were part of this system of beliefs.

1   Men and women were inherently different. Their sexual differences resulted in opposite, though complementary, personalities and abilities.

2   Women were nurturing, moral and altruistic; men were rational, competitive and individualistic.

3   Women's behaviour was biologically determined, whereas men's behaviour was under their intellectual control.

4.   Women's sphere was private, home and family; men's sphere was public, the world beyond the confines of the family.

5.   It was important for the maintenance of social stability that women's primary role remain the home and family.

The notion of different norms and expectations associated with separate spheres for men and women provided the rationale for women to extend the boundaries of their domestic sphere. Women used the ideology of sexual differences to raise female consciousness, to justify a public role for themselves and to establish a network of female friendships, all of which facilitated the development of social work. Historically, professionalism was based on a male ethos (Abbott and Wallace, 1990; Hearn, 1985; Glazer and Slater, 1987). Consequently, the nineteenth-century professional woman was continually described in reference to men. Adherence to the ideology of gender differences did not promote recognition and respect for women's diversity. Nor did it advance the need for collective action to promote women's equality in the profession of social work. Indeed, as Baines (1993, p. 67) states, "women in social work have been more conservative than their sisters in nursing and teaching and they have tended to work toward equality in a more individual way."

The following chapter will examine the way that nineteenth-century ideas about women continue to affect the social work profession. While this ideology was applied to a broad population of women, the writer has confined the discussion to nineteenth-century upper and middle class women.

Introduction

During the nineteenth century, Canada experienced rapid and profound social change moving from a predominantly rural, agricultural society to an increasingly industrialized, urban society with a diverse ethnic mix (Cook and Mitchinson, 1976; Prentice et al., 1988; Brown and Cook, 1976; Gill and Gannon, 1987). The impact of these changes caused great concern for all Canadians about the future of their country (Valverade, 1991).

Historically sexual differences between men and women were balanced by their economic interdependence (Silverman, 1984; Gannon and Gill, 1987). Urbanization, industrialization and mechanization changed the occupational structure of society for men and for women. As business and industry took men away from the home, women were separated from the world of work and money. Many continued toiling in the home to produce goods and services for their families, but their work was not recognized because they were not wage earners. When the location and definition of work changed, women's economic role in the family decreased — varying with their social class and geographic location — and their economic dependency increased. Although single women were employed as factory workers, domestics and teachers in parts of Canada, the majority of women found themselves isolated from political and economic activity. Since women's subordinate status was codified in law, they were dependent on men, whether as husbands, fathers or employers. For most of the nineteenth century, women had no legal control over property or children; they could not vote, had few educational opportunities and they were considered intellectually inferior to men. The *Queen's College Journal* noted in 1876:

> That women's...proper sphere...is the domestic circle. Their highest duties they owe to the family...therefore her education should be practical, fitting her to govern her household...her mind should be cultivated, but her mental culture should not be regarded as what is distinctively intellectual. (Cook and Mitchinson, 1977)

The decline in the value attributed to women's economic contributions to the family and society was compensated by the importance attached to her qualities as a woman. They were designated as the stabilizing force in society. Social stability and progress depended upon a sexual division of labour: women's responsibility was to fulfil the role of wife and mother. It was their sacred mission to preserve the home.

Women were expected to set a good example for men. It was assumed that their voluntary submission to authority in the home and church would be emulated by men in the larger society. The moral values they taught in the home were to compensate for the commercial and competitive values in society. Fulfilment of women's role to safeguard social stability was predicated upon their willingness to relinquish their self-interest for the good of others. Success then inevitably required that women internalize dependence as a style of interaction.

Women were expected to be pious, pure, submissive and domestic. They were to find their true vocation as wives and mothers. Men were expected to be acquisitive, competitive, less religious and the economic "breadwinners." Men attempted to be moral, but the demands of their biology and of the economic world made it difficult without the morality and stability that only women in the home could provide. "A wife will do good to her husband by encouraging him to holiness and virtue, and warning him against sin." (Cook and Mitchinson, 1977, p. 30).

The ideology of true womanhood stressed a marked dichotomy between home (the woman's sphere) and the outside world (the man's sphere). As long as women confined themselves to their "proper realm," they were considered "ladies" and accorded the respect of society. If women dared to transgress these boundaries to undertake a profession they were looked upon as "unsexed," strong-minded, perfectly horrid, coarse and unnatural (Cook and Mitchinson, 1977, p. 136).

Women's maternal nature, their loving kindness, gentleness and moral piety equipped them to be a moral inspiration to others; their power lay in the ability to influence others by persuasion and personal example. If others did not respond appropriately, their duty was simply to try harder. Constant forgiveness, self-sacrifice and patience were essential to success. An inevitable drawback of women's sex role was a tendency to be self-critical. Any shortfall was interpreted as the woman's personal failure. Although they were expected to offer patience and empathy to others, it was often difficult for a woman to extend such feelings to herself. As long as women accepted the role ascribed to them, that of instilling morality, self-control and selflessness, they were acting to preserve the values most under threat in society. Both religion and popular literature reinforced the conviction that men and women were polar opposites with dramatically different, though complementary, characteristics. The religious emphasis on domestic virtues reflected and reinforced the cult of true womanhood. Christian virtues became female virtues: humility, piety, charity and dedication of self to others.

Women and Social Reform

Reinforcing the importance of their moral duty and their ability to reform the family gave many women a rationale to enter public life. A substantial number took their moral mandate seriously and went out to improve the world. Beginning in the nineteenth century, women became involved in developing Sunday schools and a multitude of benevolent associations. They expanded their sphere of activity to include reforming drunkards and prostitutes, and improving health, housing and working conditions for women. Before the end of the century, women operated welfare systems in many cities and towns across Canada (Burt, Code and Dorney, 1993; Prentice et al., 1988; Gannon and Gill, 1987).[1]

The cult of domesticity and true womanhood was an ambivalent ideology that simultaneously devalued and elevated women. By assuming that all women were the same, it acted to unify women and to confirm their satisfaction with their sex. Religion and female voluntary associations encouraged the development of friendships among women. Although the groups and associations never represented all Canadian women, a "bond of womanhood" developed (Cott, 1977; Prentice et al., 1988; Burt et al., 1993). Women saw themselves as having a common purpose and mission.

Evolutionary Theory and Social Work

The popularization of an evolutionary theory of society, Social Darwinism, applied the concept of survival of the fittest to the human realm. It asserted that hard work, acquisitiveness, individualism and self-reliance were male virtues that led to economic success. By equating economic achievement with moral virtue,

Social Darwinism also led to the belief that poverty could be attributed to moral inadequacy and failure.

Evolutionary theory provided a scientific rationale for the belief in discrete spheres for men and women. It attributed to biology the role and characteristics ascribed to women. The laws of nature dictated that women were nurturing, altruistic, emotional, delicate and dependent. The same rules of nature determined that men were independent, economically driven, competitive and strong. They were naturally the rivals of other men. Conversely, biology dictated that women's potential for motherhood made them naturally noncompetitive, passive and dependent. They possessed greater capacity for tenderness and nurturing and were less selfish than men. Such biologically determined attributes identified them as the natural caregivers of society.

Biological differences were reflected in mental functions. In the evolutionary hierarchy — ranging from instinct to reason — women ranked above children but below men. Since they were closer to nature, their nervous systems were more primitive, suitable for expressing emotion, sentiment and sympathy. "Intuition, rapid perception and perhaps imitation are more strongly marked in women. These, of course, are more characteristic of the lower races and state of civilization" (Agontino, 1977, p. 250). Others noted that equality, whatever it is before God, in no way implies the parity of roles in society ... woman by her very sex, by her physical structure and her moral qualities, by her tastes, talents and tendancies absolutely differs from man ... and results in a difference in their duties (Prentice et al., 1988, p. 145).

Although women were opposed to the determinism of Social Darwinism and the conception of society based upon individual competition, they did not reject the evolutionary notion that women had evolved differently from men. They assumed women's natural altruism, self-sacrifice and concern for the less fortunate could counterbalance male competitiveness and acquisitiveness. Their influence was expected to bring order and morality to a society where the danger and disorder accompanying social change seemed to threaten social progress. When nineteenth-century social reformers claimed that women's moral power was essential to social progress, they did not mean that women were to have an equal social position; they were to play a complementary role. Women were not men's equal; they were their "better" half. She was cautioned not to forget her position as the complement of man and warned not to "usurp the place of man" (Cook and Mitchinson, 1977, p. 9). Darwin's theory tended to underestimate the validity of the Bible and undermined the authority of the church (Cook, 1985). The church had to become more socially responsible. Women were thus particularly suited to become the volunteers in Christian charity. As guardians of the home their natural charitable and benevolent abilities could be applied to society's problems (Prentice et al., 1988, pp. 168-69).

The Dual Beginnings of Social Work

By the late nineteenth century in Canada, the wastefulness of uncoordinated charity and the turmoil in the cities were subjects of much public concern (Valverade, 1991; Prentice et al., 1988). The need for solutions to some of the social problems in the cities resulted in the development of voluntary charity societies and settlement houses in the 1880s and 1890s. Social work evolved from these two organized forms of benevolence. The goals, philosophy and methods each employed to deal with social and human problems differed somewhat, but there were several commonalities. Both were attempts to provide an organized response to the human need engendered by rapid social change. Both were derived from English models, and advanced by middle- and upper-class men and women who wanted to be of service to others. Neither approach questioned the view that men and women possessed different but complementary abilities and interests.

Settlers and charity workers in Canada believed that problems in society could be solved in different ways. One approach was to attempt to change the structure of society to make it more equitable. The alternative approach was to work with people with problems, helping them cope with the existing environment and make better use of resources. Settlement workers, whether religious or secular, tended to represent the first approach; charity workers the second. Differences in philosophy and method between these approaches were eventually to become a source of controversy in social work. It left the profession with a legacy of unresolved conflict: Was the purpose of social work to change the individual or to change the social environment? (Abbott and Wallace, 1990; Moscovitz and Abbott, 1987).

The charity approach in Canada was based on religion and tended to explain human behaviour in moral terms. Poverty was not caused solely by environmental factors; a lack of character and a weak will were also contributing factors. Since poverty was self-induced, it followed that self-help was the only possible remedy. Alms-giving exacerbated pauperism by destroying the work ethic, creating a dependency and weakening the moral fibre of the individual. Charity dispensed not monetary aid but advice. If absolutely essential, food and fuel were provided, but only after careful investigation. Women in charity societies often differentiated between the worthy poor and the unworthy poor. "Promiscuous alms giving is fatal ... it is the patent process for the manufacture of paupers out of worthlessness and improvidence" (Moscovitch and Albert, 1981, p. 68).

In their attempts to make philanthropy scientific, charity workers emphasized strong leadership, efficient management and the coordination of existing welfare services. Fact-gathering for each case was considered the scientific way to ensure that only the worthy poor and not "imposters" received material aid. There was also much concern that the poor were seeking aid from multiple charities (Valverade, 1991, p. 159). Canadian charity organizations accepted the conventional nineteenth-century belief that it was women's moral obligation to relieve poverty by reforming the poor. A "good woman's" influence could modify the attitudes, behaviour and lifestyle of the poor.

Most settlement houses were run by men and staffed by women. Settlement workers attempted to engage the poor in cooperative community development efforts. They avoided religious preaching and charity. Settlements were established in major Canadian cities: Montreal had three, Ottawa and Fort William one, and Toronto two (Valverade, 1991, p. 142). Settlement workers believed that voluntary sharing of intellectual and material resources and communication among different classes of people were the keys to improving society. Through the experience of living and working in the cities, secular settlers recognized that it was not character defects in the individual that caused poverty. The causes lay in the social and economic conditions over which the individual had little or no control. The religious missions, unlike the secular settlements, did not attribute poverty solely to the social and environmental conditions of urban life. Under church authority, relying on volunteer women to deliver services, they provided a range of services to poor families and disadvantaged groups. However, the missions continued to discriminate between the respectable working-class poor and the "wrecks of the slum" (Valverade, 1991, p. 143).

The evolutionary ideology of divergent abilities between men and women helped establish social work as an occupation particularly suited to women. It validated the belief that women had a natural ability to help others. As women developed the profession of social work, most did not question the concept of sexual differences. Rather, they considered the abilities and characteristics associated with their sphere an asset. As a result, women in the social work profession conformed to a secular interpretation of the cult of true womanhood: domestic, benevolent, self-sacrificing and exhibiting superior morality.

When women justified their concern with social reform as social housekeeping it reduced social criticism directed at women as they moved beyond the private domestic realm. However, it also promoted an underestimation and misrepresentation of the analytical, organizational and management skills that women in Canada employed to effect radical changes in society and to create the profession of social work. Consequently, women's reform endeavours have been characterised as "social housekeeping by Protestant nuns" or as maternal feminism (O'Neil, 1969; Rothman, 1978; Baines et al., 1991; Prentice, et al., 1988).

These ideas meant that women in social work would play an important but secondary role in the professional hierarchy. As society became more bureaucratized, scientific and professionally orientated, women in social work who aspired to professional status soon found that separate and different was not equal.

Implications for the Current Status of Women in Social Work

In the past, few questioned the predominance of females in social work or the notion that women were "naturally" suited for the "helping profession." Today, however, the large number of women in the field and their orientation to service are often viewed as the primary reasons for the low status of the profession (Etzioni, 1969; Kravetz, 1976, 1982).

The major difficulty that women inherited from the past and encounter in social work today is the persistent belief in dualisms. Reason and analytic thinking are considered superior to emotion and intuition. As Walters, Carter, Papp and Silverstein (1988) suggest, intuition and reason are inseparable. To dichotomize these modes of being and of understanding ... in our gender defined society will lead to a referencing that devalues women. Numerous studies have found that all occupations in which women predominate enjoy less prestige, status and authority than male fields (Armstrong and Armstrong, 1986; Abbott and Wallace, 1990). While women constitute the majority of students in schools of social work in Canada, as well the majority of practitioners in the field (Armstrong and Armstrong, 1986; Ralph, 1992; Sharp, 1992), men occupy a disproportionate share of high-level positions (Epstein, 1988; Gould and Kim, 1976; Williams, 1992). Men predominate in senior faculty posts, agency management, community organizations and policy-formulating positions (Williams, 1992). They tend to concentrate in intellectual, analytical, policy-making and administrative areas of the profession; women are concentrated in the nurturing, affective, one-to-one practice areas. As a result, "women as direct service professional workers have limited autonomy and control over their work and limited influence over policy and resource allocation" (Baines et al., 1991, p. 68). The fact that success is generally defined by academic and administrative expertise rather than practice means that the so-called female profession is often led by men.

Current research indicates little support for sex differences in achievement, motivation, risk taking and task persistence — characteristics typically associated with successful professional attainment. The conviction persists that men and women manifest diametrically different characteristics (Mackie, 1991; Weick, 1980; Broverman, Broverman, Clarkson and Rosenkrantz, 1972). Men are assumed to be rational, independent and achievement oriented, while women are assumed to be affiliative, expressive and intuitive. "The power or nurturance is associated with the female private sphere" (Abbott and Wallace, 1990, p. 60).

The stereotypical female qualities of expressiveness, nurturing and person-oriented modes of behaviour are generalized to the profession. Social work is a sex-typed occupation, an occupation that a large majority are of one sex, and there is a normative expectation that this is as it should be (Merton, 1970). However, stereotypical male qualities are more highly valued. This dualistic thinking promotes the assumption that women in social work need not be as dedicated, ambitious or serious about their careers and their studies as their male counterparts. It leads to the belief that the claims of home and family will take precedence over women's career goals (Mackie, 1991; Armstrong and Armstrong, 1986). A second consequence of dualistic thinking leads to the belief that men must be recruited to improve the profession's status (Baines, et al., 1991; Gripton, 1974; Struthers, 1987). It is expected that the presence of men will "defeminize" the field and make it more scientific and intellectual. However, "the expectation that equality ... will prevail as men enter fields traditionally filled by women has proven to be false ..." (Baines, et al., 1991, p. 66).

Summary

The institutionalization of the concept of separate spheres in the profession meant that many women internalized the nineteenth-century American norms and values assigned them by the dominant culture. They implicitly acknowledged that their expertise was a natural consequence of their biological differences from men. This rationale has not served the cause of women's professional equality. By declaring social work an occupation particularly suitable for women, they found themselves confined to a career that reinforced the belief that they should occupy a different realm than men. Their professions where related to the "moral economy," the not-for-profit sector of society (Conway, p. 1). Consequently few women gained access to professional, economic or political sources of power and influence.

The concentration of women in social work was attributed to natural specialization rather than to artificial discrimination. Women were unable to free themselves from their historically ascribed role to nurture and protect others. They were expected to meet others' needs before their own by humanizing hospitals and health care, public policy and the provision of human services. Fear of sanctions directed against them, or against others for whom they were responsible, served to keep the majority of women from becoming advocates on their own behalf. Women were caught in "the compassion trap" (Adams, 1971).

Equating women's differences from men with inferiority meant any articulation of sexual differences or sex solidarity risked reconfirming the sex prejudice professional women sought to obliterate. Professional women social workers had to prove they were not irrational, emotional and subjective. Women thus sought to assimilate, to be like male professionals.

The professional credo that women would be judged by individual merit and objective standards was very attractive to those in one of the most sex-segregated occupations. Thus women did achieve high status in the field. Their individual success, however, did not bring into being programs for positive change in the position of women in the profession.

As long as professional women depended upon male criteria to define the route to achievement, this required that they demonstrate that they were unlike women. Professional success was based on adoption of the lifestyle, language and occupational skills of the dominant group: a male referent. Despite the efforts of women in social work to become professional, biologically and socially based ideas, which historically confined them to a separate sphere, continued to adversely affect their efforts to gain professional equality.

These ideas eventually led to inevitable and irreconcilable conflicts for women in social work. As long as society maintained different and conflicting standards for women and the professions, female social workers simultaneously had to conform to traditional social norms for women and to a model of professionalism that reflected traditional male benchmarks. Their dilemma remained: if women's differences from men made them more nurturing and sensitive to the needs of others and their claim to professional status was based upon their female expertise, then they could not claim that their profession was the same as the male profession. Conversely, if they were the same as men, it followed that their expertise was based upon knowledge and skill, then how could they account for their continuing inequality — other than as personal choice or inadequacy?

"Difference Feminism" has always focussed on women's separate speech, organizational styles and separate value system (Wolf, 1993). "Difference Feminism" assumes nurturing, intuition, emotionality and a focus on attachment (Gilligan, 1982; Miller, 1986). "Difference Feminism" has not constituted a force for institutional and personal changes to promote women's equality. In contrast, Wolf recommends "Power Feminism," which denies any assumptions about special abilities based on gender and emphasizes the collective power of women as a group. The effective practice of social work needs to be directed by Wolf's "Power Feminism."

The double consciousness of oneself as a woman and as a professional was the legacy of the nineteenth-century presupposition about the different temperaments and social roles of men and women. Only when women in social work recognize the destructive and limited perception of historically based gender differences can they attain equality for themselves and others.

Endnotes

1   During the nineteenth century, women organized the Women's Missionary Societies, the Women's Christian Temperence Union (the WCTU) the National Council of Women, The Dominican Women's Enfranchisement Association, National Council of Jewish Women, the YWCA and the Victoria Order of Nurses. Armour, M. and P. Stanton (eds.). (1992). *Canadian Women in History: A Chronology*. Toronto: Green Dragon Press.

References

Abbott, P. and Wallace, C. (eds.). 1990. *The Sociology of the Caring Professions*. Philadelphia: The Falmer Press.

Adams, M. 1971. "The Compassion Trap," in Gornick, V. and Moran, B. (eds.), *Women in Sexist Society Studies in Power and Powerlessness*. New American Library, p. 152. New York.

Agontino, R. 1977. *History of Ideas on Women: A Source Book*. New York: Putnam and Sons.

Armour, M. and Stanton, P. 1992. *Canadian Women in History. A Chronology*, 2nd edition. Toronto: Green Dragon Press.

Armstrong, P. and Armstrong, H. 1986. *The Double Ghetto Canadian Women and Their Segregated Work*. Toronto: McClelland and Stewart.

Baines, C., Evans, P. and Neysmith, S. (eds.). 1991. *Women Caring. Feminist Perspectives on Social Welfare*. Toronto: McClelland and Stewart.

Bernard, J. 1981. *The Female World*. New York: The Free Press.

Broverman, I. K., Broverman, D. M., Clarkson, F. E., Rosenkrantz, P. S. and Vogel, S. R. 1970. "Sex Role Stereotypes and Clinical Judgements of Mental Health." *Journal of Consulting and Clinical Psychology*. 34: 1-7.

Broverman, I. K., Broverman, D. M., Clarkson, F. E. and Rosenkrantz, P. S. 1972. "Sex Role Stereotypes: A Current Appraisal." *Journal of Social Issues*. 28: 3, 59-78.

Brown, R. and Cook, R. 1976. *Canada 1896-1921: A Nation Transformed*. Toronto: McClelland and Stewart.

Burt, S., Code, L. and Dorney, L. (eds.). 1993. *Changing Patterns. Women in Canada*, 2nd edition. Toronto: McClelland and Stewart.

Cook, R. 1985. *The Regenerators. Social Culticism in Late Victorian English Canada*. Toronto: University Press.

Cook, R. and Mitchinson, W. (eds.). 1977. *Women's Proper Sphere. Women's Place in Canadian Society*. Toronto: Oxford University Press.

Cott, N. 1977. *The Bonds of Womanhood: Woman's Sphere in New England, 1730-1835*. New Haven: Yale University Press.

Epstein, C. 1988. *Deceptive Distinctions Sex, Gender and the Social Order*. New Haven: Yale University Press.

Etzioni, A. (ed.). 1969. *The Semi-professions and Their Organization: Teachers, Nurses and Social Workers*. New York: The Free Press.

Gilligan, C. 1982. *In a Different Voice: Psychological Theory and Womens' Development*. Cambridge, Mass.: Harvard University Press.

Glazer, P. and Slater, M. 1987. *Unequal Colleagues: The Entrance of Women into the Professions, 1890-1945*. New Brunswick, NJ: Rutgers University Press.

Gould, K. H. and Kim, B. L. 1976. "Salary Inequities Between Men and Women in Schools of Social Work." *Journal of Education for Social Work*. 12: 50-55.

Gripton, J. 1974. "Sexism in Social Work: Male Takeover of a Female Profession." *Social Worker*. (Summer) 42: 78-89.

Hearn, J. 1985. "Patriarchy, Professionalism and the Semi-professions," in Ingerson, Clare (ed.), *Women and Social Policy*. McMillan, London.

Kravetz, D. 1976. "Sexism in a Woman's Profession." *Social Work.* (November) 21: 6, 421-427.

Kravetz, D. 1982. "An Overview of Content on Women for the Social Work Curriculum." *Journal of Education for Social Work.* (Spring) 18: 42-49.

Mackie, M. 1991. *Gender Relations in Canada.* Toronto: Butterworths.

Merton, R.K. 1970. In Epstein, C.F., *Women's Place: Options and Limits in Professional Careers.* Berkeley, California: University of California Press.

Miller, J.B. 1986. *Toward a New Psychology of Women.* Boston: Beacon Press.

O'Neil, W. 1969. *Everyone Was Brave: A History of Feminism in America.* New York Times Book Co.

Prentice, A., Bourne, P., Brandt, G., Light, B., Mitchinson, W. and Black, N. 1988. *Canadian Woman: A History.* Toronto: Harcourt, Brace, Jovanavich.

Ralph, D. 1992. "Gender and Social Work Faculty." Fact sheet #1, Canadian Association of Schools of Social Work.

Rothman, S. 1978. *Women's Proper Place. A History of Changing Ideals and Practices 1870-present.* New York: Basic Books.

Sharp, A. 1992. "Distribution of Student Body by Gender, Program and Enrollment." Fact sheet #4, Canadian Association of Schools of Social Work.

Silverman, E. 1984. *The Last Best West. Women on the Alberta Frontier, 1880-1930.* Montreal: Eden Press.

Struthers, J. 1987a. "Lord Give Us Men. Women and Social Work in English Canada, 1918-1953," in Moscovitch, A. and J. Albert (eds.), *The Benevolent State: The Growth of Welfare in Canada.* Toronto: Garamond Press.

Struthers, J. 1987b. "A Profession in Crisis: Charlotte Whitten and Canadian Social Work in the 1930s," in Moscovitch, A. and J. Albert (eds.), *The Benevolent State: The Growth of Welfare in Canada.* Toronto: Garamond Press.

Valverade, M. 1991. *The Age of Light, Soap, and Water: Moral Reform in English Canada, 1885-1925.* Toronto: McClelland and Stewart.

Walters, M., Carter, B., Papp, P. and Silverstein, O. 1988. *The Invisible Web: Gender Patterns in Family Relationships.* New York: Guilford Press.

Weick, A. and Vandiver, S. (eds.). 1980. *Women, Power, and Change.* Washington, D.C.: National Association of Social Workers.

Welter, B. 1966. "The Cult of True Womanhood, 1820-1860." *American Quarterly.* (Summer) 18: 151-174.

Williams, C. 1992. "The Glass Escalator: Hidden Advantages For Men in the `Female Professions'." *Social Problems.* (August) 39: 253-265.

Wolf, N. 1994. *Fire with Fire. The New Female Power and How to Use It.* Toronto: Random House.

Chapter II
An Historical Overview of Sexism in Medical Practice

Darlene Simpson

The purpose of this chapter is to explore the roots of sexism that exist in today's medical practices. The historical role of women as healers and women as patients needs to be examined in order to develop a more thorough understanding of the health issues that confront women today. Historically, the practice of medicine has been granted legitimacy under the authority of science. Some would say that medicine has acted, and continues to act, as a force of social control oppressive to women. It is hoped that this chapter will shed light on how the objective process of science has been inseparable from the subjective observers who were influenced by the prevailing norms of their day and how these scientific observers, a relatively small, white male, group, defined what is normal for women (Hubbard, 1990).

Sexism and patriarchy are widespread in the medical care system today. Sexism being the tendency to construct stereotypes based on gender and patriarchy being simply male dominance over women resulting in males being situated in the highest stratum of every social institution (Mackie, 1991), including economic, political, legal, family, educational, religious and medical systems within society. Much of the literature studying sexism in health care is decidedly feminist in perspective. Since the onset of the women's movement, it is apparent that feminists have been the group most interested in pursuing the sociopolitical history of women in medicine. In this chapter, following the historical role of women as healers and patients, a brief look at the impact of the women's movement on women's health care, women in medical practice today and the implications of reproductive technology will precede the implications for social workers in health care settings.

Women as Healers

Women have long been participating as healers of the sick, however, their healing role has historically been sabotaged, discredited and has even fallen under persecution by male-dominated society. Documents dating back to 300 BC indicate that women were participating as healers. However, men's tradition to curb women attaining status as healers has an equally long history. One Greek woman named Agnodice was accused in 300 BC of practising obstetrics and gynaecology without being formally trained, though she had attended classes disguised as a male (Webb, 1986).

Women were blatantly barred from healing in the Middle Ages. During the antiempirical times of the middle ages, female healers, called sorceresses, discovered medicinal remedies that made healing possible. The sorceress learned from her observations and was even known to dissect corpses to examine anatomy. They, and the "sagas" and "wise women" who followed them, were available to treat the poor, especially women and children, who were not likely to come near "professional" medical aid as early physicians tended only to treat the upper classes. By using herbs and nurturing the body back to strength they cured many. Their methods were rejected by physicians whose medical procedures were based on fourth-century Galenic, theory which adhered to the belief that illness was caused solely by an imbalance in the body's four fluids (blood, phlegm, back bile and yellow bile). Thus, the atrocious practice of blood letting ensued, which in itself killed many patients.

In 1527, Philippus Aureolus Paracelsus, a great Renaissance physician, burned his medical books in protest at the University of Basil, claiming the information contained within was useless. He attributed all his medical success to knowledge he had obtained from the "sagas" or "wise women" of his day who had much experience curing the poor and sick. Unfortunately, even with the support of Philippus Aureolus Paracelsus, such women were being unjustly persecuted for their knowledge. The infamous witch hunts, based on the *Malleus Malefircarum*, from 1479-1735 are still remembered with horror today. The *Malleus Malefircarum* (or Hammer of Witches) became the Catholic Church's official guide to witch-hunting wherein helping and healing were in themselves considered evidence of witchcraft. The wise women or witches who healed may have used magical remedies such as amulets and charms, but they had also developed natural healing methods from years of experience. The book, *Libre Simplicis Medicinae*, for example, written by St. Hildegarde of Bingen (AD 1098-1178), listed the healing properties of 213 plants and 55 trees as remedies (Ehrenreich and English, 1979), several of which are used today. However, the Catholic Church of the fourteenth century claimed that any woman who could cure the sick without having studied was a witch and must die. Midwives were especially suspect because it was believed they participated in the birth experience to get their hands on after-birth products to be used in heathenistic rituals. (Women were considered particularly susceptible to be witches because it was believed they were vulnerable to consorting with the devil in a sexual way.) The most reliable estimates indicate that about 9 million people were executed as witches during the fifteenth to seventeenth centuries (Corea, 1977).

Before the witch-hunts ensued, efforts had been made to eliminate women from practising medicine. The literate woman who might treat the upper classes was most likely to have her efforts opposed. In 1322, Jacoba Felicie, who was known to cure her patients, was brought to trial by the Faculty of Medicine at the University of Paris for practising medicine without proper training. Yet ironically, the gentlemanly profession of physicians at that time was, in many respects, based more on myth than the healing practices of the wise women. University trained physicians spent most of their training studying philosophical and theological issues, as well as Galenic theory. With little experimentation, and no anatomical observation, physicians in competition with the "witch-healers" prescribed leeches and a host of absurd remedies. For example, leprosy was often treated with the "broth made of the flesh of a black snake caught in a dry land among stones" (Ehrenreich and English, 1979, p.38).

In colonial America, there were no, or very few, doctors available, so women again took on the role of healers as "domestic practitioners." This practice went on uninterrupted until 1765 when doctors wanted the medical profession to exclude unlicensed practitioners. At this time laws began to be passed in various states that excluded the unlicensed (women) from practising medicine. In Canada, the first step to regulate medical practitioners came in 1788, in an act "to prevent persons practising physic and surgery within the Province of Quebec, or midwifery in the towns of Montreal or Quebec without a licence" (Mitchinson and McGinnis, 1988, p. 12). In 1795, the legislature of Upper Canada followed suit by allowing only licensed physicians to practice in the colony. Medical practices were still based on treatments attempting to balance the body's four fluids. Blood letting was common, and doctors continued to bleed and purge their patients with leeches and surgical knives. Prescribing large doses of drugs like nitre and calomel (a mercurous laxative) was also common. It goes without saying, that many doctors did more harm than good to their patients. These doctors came to be known as allopaths, they were exclusively male and upper class. In their drive to exclude unlicensed practitioners, they aimed their energies at disqualifying the competing sects of the day, which included irregular healers, referred to as "quacks," who subscribed to various theories. For example, the Thomsonians (herbalists and feminists), the Eclectics (used what they considered the most sensible treatment) and the Homeopaths (who concentrated on building up the patient's natural strength or immune system to fight illness) were considered dangerous and unscientific in their approach. However, during the 1830s and 40s American irregulars fought to repeal the licensing laws and won. They succeeded largely because the general public shared their hostility toward the doctors. The average person was offended that the profession had become so elite, and without reasonable competition their incomes were allowed to remain high. So, due to the general public's jealousy and resentment, the licensing law was revoked in the 1830s. Women began to re-establish their roles as healers from 1850 to 1870. Separate medical schools for women were set up, 19 in the U.S. between 1850 and 1895, as established programs continued to reject women. In 1850, the Female Medical College of Pennsylvania was established and in 1878 the Pennsylvania Hospital admitted women into training. Women in Canada were making their way south for further education. Until Augusta Stowe-Gullen completed her education in Toronto in 1883, all female physicians practising in the Dominion had trained outside of the country, usually in American or British schools. Doctors Emily Howard Jennings Stowe (New York Medical College for Women, 1867) and Jennie Kidd Trout (Women's Medical College of Philadelphia, 1875) were the first female physicians licensed to practice in Canada.

Jennie Kidd Trout and Emily Howard Stowe, doctors and friends who eventually became rivals, both initiated the first medical training programs for women in Canada. At first Doctors Trout and Stowe were rejected by the Toronto male doctors, even after offering $10,000 of their own money. Dismayed, Trout turned to Queen's University in Kingston, initiating the establishment of the Women's Medical College in Kingston, pledging $200 a year of her own money for the first five years. Support for the Kingston college was justified, in part, by the belief that women physicians would improve domestic hygiene. Stowe, drawing more "feminist" supporters than Trout, persisted until the Women's Medical College affiliated with the University of Toronto was to be realized. Both medical colleges opened in October of 1883. Unfortunately, the opening of the women's colleges was not a purely progressive move. Due to dwindling funds, Queen's shut down their program from 1893 to 1943. The Ontario Medical College for Women in Toronto shut down in 1905 when the University of Toronto agreed to admit women to its own medical courses. The number of female doctors rose from 76 in 1891 to 196 in 1911, but by 1921 there were only 152 female doctors in Canada (Strong-Boag, 1981).

Women's inclusion into the medical realm has never been an easy one. Male doctors bitterly opposed the admission of women into medicine. Many barricades proposed in the form of scientific reasoning were erected to exclude them. Some so called "scientific" arguments included theories proving women's naturally delicate, weak and inferior physical nature. Also, it was considered ludicrous for a woman to abandon her ordained role of homemaker and mother to compete with men. Her female duties would render her highly unavailable for professional service. And if not her duties, menstruation would disable her: "The physiological peculiarities of women even in single life, and the disorders consequent on them, can not fail frequently to interfere with the regular discharge of her duties as physician in constant attendance on the sick" (Corea, 1977, p. 26).

Not only were women delicate and unavailable, they would excite male patients sexually. In 1881, the *London Lantern* mockingly described the possible dynamic between a female doctor listening to the heart of a prospective male patient: "eyes and rosebud mouth would be looking right in his face and her wavy hair would be scattered all around theirs, getting tangled in the buttons of his nightshirt, don't you suppose his heart would get in about twenty extra beats to the minute? Rather!" (Corea, 1977, p.8).

Any woman who expected to work with male patients was labelled sexually perverted and unnaturally curious — which says nothing degrading, of course, to the decency of male physicians who attend women! Even as late as 1974, a female intern was not allowed to be present because a male's genitals were exposed during a medical exam.[1] Others argued that men were afraid of the competition, were threatened by the thought of economically independent women and were concerned that the entrance of female physicians into the profession would drive men out.

During the late nineteenth and early twentieth centuries, several crippling events took place in the U.S., especially concerning the transformation of female medical schools into co-educational schools, which eventually again led to the elimination of women from medical education. Co-ed medical schools quickly shut down and second-rate schools had vital funding cut off after a 1910 medical report claimed funds were needed for male allopaths. Irregular schools were prevented from competing without their financial base.

The first American woman to enter an allopath school was Elizabeth Blackwell, and this was done in the guise of a joke. She was not expected to remain, but she graduated in 1849 with honours in every course (except she was not admitted to courses on women's diseases!) and, after serving her internship in Europe, opened her own school called the New York Infirmary for Women and Children (which was eventually taken over by men). The first known Canadian woman to be a doctor was Dr. James Miranda Stuart Barry, an excellent doctor and surgeon from Britain, who for more than 40 years was believed to be a man. She came to Canada as the Inspector-General for Hospitals for both Upper and Lower Canada in 1857. The first officially recognized female doctor in Canada was Emily Howard Jennings Stowe. In 1856, after having already been appointed a school principal, she applied to the University of Toronto but was turned down. Canada was not yet admitting women into medical schools. Eventually she graduated from the New York College of Medicine for Women. Her daughter, Augusta Stowe, was the first Canadian woman to receive a medical degree in Canada, in 1883.

Well into the twentieth century, sex discrimination continued to be rampant in the admissions screening process to enter prominent schools. If women claimed they wanted to eventually marry and have children they were considered potential drop outs. If they were single they were considered unnatural women. Female medical students were really in a catch-22 situation. They were expected to be passive and invisible. Their inquires in class were either ignored or turned into jokes and given degrading responses by equating procedures with stereotypical feminine activities such as baking bread, for example. Men expressed uneasiness about being in the presence of an intelligent woman. In 1974, a female physician who served on an intern selection committee cited several written examples of some of the reasons why certain female students were referred: "She has no hang-ups sometimes associated with female physicians" or "Her intelligence stands out...but does not antagonize her male colleagues" and finally "She is completely unintimidating despite her obvious fine intellect" (Corea, 1977, p.38). Women were expected to act in stereotypic ways — flirtatious, admiring and servile. Well past the mid 1900s, they were seen solely as daughters, wives, mothers or playmates. If women were not passive and responsive to men's advances they were often labelled castrating or hysterical. If they were, they were unprofessional. After all, success unsexed a women in the eyes of her male contemporaries. Women also beat on other women. Sexism in women is not surprising. Women had internalized men's negative image of them, and thus it followed women would undervalue other women. Arguments that women only went to medical school to find a husband were common. If not interested in finding a mate, she was considered sexless and dateless. Estelle Ramsey describes the stereotype shared by both sexes of a female medical student in 1971 by typically depicting her as a "horse-faced, flat chested female in suphose who supplements her sex starvation in a passionate embrace of the New England Journal of Medicine" (Corea, 1977, p.31).

No provisions were made for pregnancy. Pregnancy was considered unprofessional, so new mothers risked their health to return quickly to work, fearing they would lose their place if they did not. Well into the 1970s, hospitals provided no sleeping quarters for female medical students and the lounge was considered a men's club where women were not welcome. Tired of fighting, women largely ended up taking the paths of least resistance by going into the fields of paediatrics, psychiatry and anaesthesiology. In short, female medical students had to go into fields where they were most likely to get internships and where they endured the least amount of rejection. This streamlining continues today. Interestingly, gynaecology, considered the field representative of female health, is still largely dominated by men.

Even in the 1990s gender bias is evident in human anatomy textbook illustrations for medical students. Female bodies are not equally represented in medical textbooks. They are depicted in only 11 per cent of standard human anatomy illustrations (Giacomini, et al., 1986). Only in the reproductive sections are women equally represented. Male bodies continue to represent the human body, perpetuating the male norm as representative for all human activity, including all physical functioning from abdominal muscles to the circulatory system, while female bodies are associated only fully with their reproductive capacity. Further, such a drastic omission of female bodies subtly suggests to upcoming doctors that female bodies are somehow not normal and contributes to the attitude that female patients are not as worthy of a doctor's time.

Since the rise of allopathy, healing was divided into care and cure. Male doctors took over the cure functions and left women to take over the care of patients. Women were far more likely to become nurses than doctors. The helping role was already accepted as feminine in nature, and nursing schools certainly erected no barriers to women. Expectedly, nurses have come to internalize and perpetuate the powerful image of the doctor as healer. Nursing activities cater first to the convenience of the doctor by fulfilling the doctors orders through a variety of tasks like giving injections and pills rather than the needs of the patient. But what benefit would the nurse have in dethroning the doctor?

> If the empowerment of the nurse means that the physician is dethroned as king of the hospital hierarchy only to be replaced by a queen, hospital workers will hardly rejoice for while doctors often see nurses as stupid underlings, nurses treat lower-paid practical nurses (LPNs) and aides just as contemptuously…. One aide explained to *Ms.* magazine: "The doctor thinks he's God; the nurse thinks she's an angel; and everyone thinks the aide is shit" (Corea, 1977, p.68).

Women as Patients

As the previous section illustrates, professional health care was divided by the 1800s when allopathy was established as the predominant and only valid school of medicine. Men were largely left to define female health problems and diseases. Many researchers interested in the field of medical history would suggest that the male-dominated medical profession came to act as a means of social control over women. Scientific descriptions of women as biological and social organisms were used to maintain sexual inequality (Hubbard, 1990). Women were "kept in their place," or rather, kept dependent on men, especially upper-class women of the Victorian era who were encouraged to be confined to their homes. The basis for treating women as the weaker, more delicate sex was confirmed in the patriarchal teachings of the Bible and so-called facts derived from scientific theory of the day. Unfortunately, yet expectedly, physicians adhered to such beliefs and contributed to them by often defining female reproductive functions as pathological conditions — consequently menstruation, pregnancy, childbirth and menopause were redefined as illness.

Women naturally began to internalize the loud and clear messages given to them by their all-knowing physicians. One view looking back on this time in history is that such expectations bred invalidism among women, especially among upper-class women because their poor female contemporaries were busy working their fingers to the bone in and out of their homes and had illnesses spreading among the urban slums to deal with as well. That poor women could bear many children and work hard proved to scientists of the day not the robust health of women but rather the animal-like qualities of the less highly evolved poor (Hubbard, 1990). In contrast, nineteenth-century-upper- and middle-class women were regarded as weak and became natural invalids, feminists would say utilizing the power of slaves. Such women were left few options outside of their role of mother and homemaker and some devoted their lives to invalidism, bedding down at every period. There was little desire for a woman to get well. Beauty and purity were measured by a woman's fragility, and some women were even known to drink arsenic to acquire a paler complexion (Clarke, 1990). Higher education was believed to damage a woman's reproductive capacity. And, sadly, many women who may have been clinically depressed were misdiagnosed and treated with further inactivity. The "rest cure" involved: "isolation in a dark room, eating a bland, boring diet of soft foods, and receiving no company except the doctor and nurse. This sensory deprivation was for the purpose of resting the brain or inducing the cessation of thought" (Clarke, 1990, p.243).

In 1887, Charlotte Perkins Gilman wrote of her experience with the "rest cure" in a story entitled "The Yellow Wallpaper." Married to a physician, her "nervous condition" and "slight hysterical tendency" was treated with phosphates, tonics and exclusion from people and work. Confined to a depressing room, with wallpaper that presented an "optic horror" to Gilman, her isolation only served to sink her deeper into depression and self-doubt.

In the nineteenth century, women's reproductive functions were considered inherently pathological and were most often blamed for women's failing health. Historically, many seemingly pathological conditions in the eyes of men were attributed to malfunctional ovaries or over-active genitals. After all, female sexuality was regarded as unwomanly and even detrimental to her reproductive capacity. Thus, removal of ovaries to cure uncontrollable lust, and a vast array of unrelated illnesses such as stomach disorders or even tuberculosis, became common in the

1800s. Doctors were known to compete with each other over the numbers of ovaries they extirpated (1500 to 2000 apiece) as if it were a sign of their virility (Corea, 1977). Methods for removal were crude, done with surgical knives or by burning, and many perfectly healthy women were denied the opportunity of having children. Surgery to replace ovaries often further botched a woman's internals. Female circumcision and clitoridectomies were performed in the U.S., reaching their peak in the 1860s, to curb the growing tide of alleged female masturbation. Reasons for performing such surgeries included physical disorders and unaccepted personality characteristics: "neurosis, insanity, abnormal menstruation and practically anything untoward in female behaviour. Among the indications were troublesomeness, eating like a ploughman, masturbation, attempted suicide, erotic tendencies, persecution mania, simple 'cussedness,' and dysmenorrhoea (painful menstruation, long held to be one consequence of masturbation)" (Ehrenreich and English, 1979, p.124).

During the 1890s, female castration was exceedingly popular. It was argued that the surgery "would make women like castrated animals — that they would become tractable, orderly, and faithful servants" (Barker-Benfield, 1972, pp. 60-61). Where scientific knowledge was not available to the extent that doctors of the day believed it was, it was replaced with myths and stereotypic beliefs. Such beliefs led to many unwarranted surgeries.

During the last part of the nineteenth century, physicians proposed differing theories to explain menstruation. Most believed that ovulation and menstruation were connected, however, it was not until the twentieth century and an understanding of the hormonal process that the timing of ovulation was fully understood. Many physicians accepted Pfluger's theory that nervous stimulation triggered menstruation, and this theory, alongside others "proving" women's natural frailty, gave justification for large numbers of physicians to oppose women's inclusion in traditionally male activities. Professor Clarke of Harvard wrote in 1873 that women should especially avoid "brain-work" between the ages of 12 and 20, in order not to overload the central nervous system from brain activity and thwart reproductive development (Bullough and Voght, 1984). Even after puberty, women were not to interfere with their process of ovulation or menstruation with any brain activity. Such beliefs were used to justify the exclusion of women time and time again from full participation in the public sphere of society.

The romance of the doctor and the ill female patient was to come to an end. Doctors had determined that women were innately sick simply due to their possession of uterus and ovaries. So sick in fact, that their deficient health due to their demanding reproductive organs was reflected in a decrease in the white, Anglo-Saxon (upper-class) population, which shrunk by half from 1800-1900

(Ehrenreich and English, 1979). By the end of the nineteenth century, the once fashionable female invalid was being suspected of malingering — that is that the legitimacy of women's suffering became questionable — and women began to face accusations of not performing their duties. Thus the gentle female invalid, who may well have used sickness as perhaps the only accepted means to avoid domestic and reproductive responsibilities, faded only to be replaced with the hysterical woman. The syndrome of hysteria, believed to be caused by the uterus, swept through North America, Britain and Europe in the late 1800s. Unlike ongoing invalidism, it was sporadic and hosted a variety of symptoms from fainting and thrashing to loss of appetite or voice. Freud came to explain both malingering and hysteria as mental illnesses. Indeed, some would say psychoanalysis was the child of hysteria (Ehrenreich and English, 1979). Interestingly, but not surprising, the common female symptoms of hysteria and fainting went out of fashion as notions about women's health began to change in the twentieth century. Yet far into the twentieth century, female biological functions, such as menstruation, pregnancy and menopause, would still be regarded as diseases. And female reproductive organs would continue to be a frontier for experimentation in the form of surgical procedures and untested drugs.

The Last Twenty Years

Today, women utilize more medical services as patients than do men (Clarke, 1990). This is not because women are more ill than men but because every stage of a woman's reproductive life is subject to medical intervention. Pregnancy and childbirth, for example, are dominated by medical care from first diagnosis to delivery. The birthing process in hospitals has changed only slightly over the years. Delivery rooms have opened up to fathers and women now have the opportunity to make more choices regarding their delivery procedure. For example, women can choose to deliver without the use of drugs (epidural), and previous Caesarian section birth mothers can request vaginal delivery. Yet births still usually take place:

> ...in hospitals, in high-tech delivery rooms, amid glaring lights in sterile conditions, and in an equally sterile emotional atmosphere, with anaesthetics to dull pain, surgery to speed delivery (whether caesarean section or merely episiotomy), forceps to change the position of the baby, and fetal monitoring to check on the progress of the baby (Clarke, 1990, p.242).

Midwifery has finally been legalized in Ontario, and professional midwifery training programs have popped up in the last years at Ryerson Polytechnical Institute in Toronto and McMaster University in Hamilton, for example. It is not surprising that Ontario, with the greatest number of obstetricians and gynaecologists, presented the greatest resistance to allowing midwives to enter the field of childbirth. This is a modern manifestation of the age-old rivalry between allopaths (male-dominated healers) and irregulars (female-dominated healers). The legalization of midwifery is a very significant step in the demedicalization of the birthing process and the increasing demand for a more human, less technical form of assistance rather than degrading, intrusive technical intervention. Doctors resisted the legalization of midwifery for the same reasons women were historically barricaded from practice — they feared the competition. Obstetricians and gynaecologists are largely male and work on a fee-for-service basis. They stand to lose a fair amount of business to the midwives. As their male brethren have historically argued, midwifery is not "professional" or "technical" in its methods, and women who use midwives were considered to be taking a high and unnecessary risk. Though midwifery was previously illegal, some women choose to have home births with trained unlicensed midwives, but that option was blatantly regarded as an irresponsible choice by the medical community. Now, licensed midwives are allowed to enter the birthing rooms of hospitals in Ontario. One would imagine the initial tension, irregulars rubbing shoulders with allopaths, will be intense.

The age-old pathologicalization of women's biological life events continues to exist. Doctors still may expect women to be undue complainers. Rather than being referred to in the historical "hysterical" term, they may be easily labelled unreasonable, hypochondriacs or neurotic, and their complaints may be passed off and not taken seriously. "A woman who goes to a doctor must turn over her body to him and at the end of the treatment she gets it back; she is entitled to no explanations, she must not ask questions nor make suggestions. Women who deviate from this role are regarded as neurotic" (Ruzek, 1978, p.77).

The label "neurotic female" is difficult to avoid, for physicians expect women to be neurotic complainers. Psychiatric theories have had tremendous influence in legitimizing sexist ideology in other branches of the medical system. Widespread use of psychoactive drugs "helps" women bring their behaviour in line with societal expectations of feminine behaviour. Thus women need not consult psychiatrists to be vulnerable to psychiatric labelling. Treating women with tranquillizers can not begin to solve the deeper problems women face, caused in part by their position in society. Women are two to three times more likely to suffer from depression than men, and although there is a biochemical basis for depression, it is strongly believed that too little emphasis continues to be placed on the reality of women's lives (Wetzel, 1994). It is known that depression is linked to lack of control, lack of recognition and feelings of helplessness. For example, mothers who stay at home are often some of our most isolated members of society and at the highest risk for mental health problems, especially depression. Women are prescribed more tranquillizers than men and are still not offered a great deal of information about the risks, addictive properties or their possible side effects. A woman prescribed tranquillizers experiences increased lethargy and is further robbed of motivation to examine her life. In short, psychotropic drugs remove symptoms without touching causes. Though substance abuse has been typically identified as a male problem, abuse of psychotropic drugs is more prevalent among women than men (Abbott, 1994). Hooked on various drugs, women become more dependent on male authorities and less able to function autonomously.

Unfortunately, women are still more likely to be viewed by their male physicians as "crazy ladies" rather than "good patients." Even battered women were more likely to get adequate treatment in U.S. emergency departments if their responses were contingent to the staff's expectations of a "good patient:" "The women have to be polite, have no discrediting attributes, and, in addition, staff members have to feel that some unfortunate event has happened to them" (Kurz, 1988, p.73). Battered women who were considered "unresponsive" or "evasive" only received a partial response. Doctors continue to consider male patients more reasonable and more likely to describe their symptoms rather than complain about them in vague terms.

One unfortunate result of male domination and medicalization of female biological development is the obvious incredible lack of knowledge women generally have of their own bodies. The rise of the women's health movement began to change the "doctor knows best — and only doctor knows" adage. Women began to learn about their own bodies. The drive of the women's health movement gave women a new control over their bodies. The American movement eventually produced a book entitled *Our Bodies, Ourselves*, which proved to be a landmark beginning for the heightening of women's awareness. The beginnings of the women's health movement took place in 1969 at a women's conference in Boston where an interested group of women met to explore a variety of relevant health issues. All in attendance shared experiences of frustration and anger toward specific doctors and the health system. They felt doctors were condescending, paternalistic, judgemental and noninformative, and further they decided they would have to learn more about their own bodies. As a result, research and papers on anatomy and physiology, sexuality, venereal disease, birth control, abortion, pregnancy, childbirth, medical institutions and the health care system were organized into health courses and lectures that were finally collected to produce *Our Bodies, Ourselves.* By March of 1971, a full-blown feminist health movement had emerged calling over 800 women to assemble in New York for the first Women's Health Conference.

Change in Canadian policy came from the many questions and resulting documentation of the American movement. During the 1970s, feminists documented the prevalence of unnecessary hysterectomies and the debilitating effects of mood-altering drugs and tranquillizers. The devastating, long-term side effects of inadequately tested drugs such as Thalidomide, DES and various birth control devices were brought to public view. Some women successfully sued major manufacturing and pharmaceutical companies as well as their doctors. Millions of women began to call for natural childbirth, home births and noninterventionist birth procedures. They even taught one another how to perform their own "internal" exams.

Drugs and devices quickly prescribed to women have a history of not being adequately tested, and female users inadvertently become part of an experimental process. The birth control pill, for example, was tested originally in Puerto Rico for a short period of time on a sample of only 132 women. This study was latter described as a "scientific scandal." The women in the test group were uninformed and used as human guinea pigs. Two or three deaths among these women were never explained or reported to the U.S. Food and Drug Administration. Barbara Seaman opened Pandora's box when she published *The Doctor's Case Against the Pill* in 1969 (Ruzek, 1978). She assembled the current body of international literature linking the pill to certain risks including clotting, strokes, sterility, decreased sexual responsiveness, cancer, heart disease, diabetes, genetic changes, jaundice, thyroid malfunction, weight gain, urinary tract infections, arthritis, skin and gum problems, depression and other medical conditions. Eventually, labels describing risks were included with prescriptions by 1977. The U.S. led the women's health movement and Canadian women have followed suit in this regard.

The DES tragedy is another example of untested drugs resulting in iatrogenic disorders. Reports of a rare form of vaginal cancer in young girls began appearing in the medical literature in 1970. Prior to this time, vaginal adenocarcinoma in adolescent girls was unknown and was unusual even in older women. Cancer experts quickly traced the cause to exposure to synthetic estrogens in utero; the mothers of the young cancer victims had been given a synthetic during pregnancy, diethylstilbestrol, commonly known as DES, to prevent miscarriage. Though the medical literature contained six scientific reports that DES was ineffective in preventing spontaneous abortions, it was actively marketed from 1941-1971. An estimated 400,000 children of DES mothers were exposed to the drug in Canada (Clarke, 1990). It was not until 1982, under the lobbying of Harriet Simand, then a

21-year-old DES victim, that Canada responded nationally to the DES tragedy by supporting DES Action Canada.

Over one million DES daughters were victims. Prognosis was poor — one-quarter of those who had developed cancer by 1978 died within 18 months of diagnosis. U.S. feminist research reports kept a watchful eye after the DES tragedy. *Her-Self, Off Our Backs, The Monthly Extract* and *The Spokeswoman* all publicized potential problems including: "dangerous levels of mercury discovered in Koromex contraceptive jelly, side effects of vaginal sprays, powerful prostaglandins as contraceptives, and carcinogenic properties of Flagyl (routinely prescribed for trichomonas, a common vaginal infection) and Tinidazole (a new rival to Flagyl)" (Ruzek, 1978, p.42).

Medical devices such as IUD's were not even under a regulatory body. Almost anyone could invent and market an IUD or other medical device without any testing — and invent them they did! During the 1960s and 70s over three million American women and another seven million worldwide received IUD's — none ever tested by a government agency. Serious complications included deaths, sterility, haemorrhage, disabling pain, unwanted pregnancy, miscarriage, ruptured tubal pregnancy, massive infection and other disorders. Thus, the horrific results of the infamous "Copper-7" did not come as a surprise. In 1974, the FDA recalled 200,000 IUDs. Many women became infected and some were not able to bear children. Women in Canada sued the manufacturers alongside American women. The Dalkon Shield IUD followed also causing pelvic inflammatory disease, blood poisoning and tubal pregnancies. It was recalled in 1974 after causing 17 deaths, yet it continued to be sold in the Third World, usually without instructions (Clarke, 1990).

In 1995, the health concerns that face contemporary women in many respects are the same issues. The medical and personal implications of hysterectomies, estrogen replacement therapy for menopause and reproductive technologies remain great concerns for women. Though the occurrence of hysterectomies declined in the 1970s when it was publicized that such surgeries were often being performed unnecessarily, the number of hysterectomies recently increased to 600,000 and 476,000 ovariectomies were performed in 1990 in the U.S. (Olson, 1994). Estrogen replacement therapy continues to battle with the concept that menopause, being a time of hormonal decline, is a disease. The benefit of estrogen in reducing osteoporosis in older women needs to be carefully weighed against the risk of cancer and yet uncertain effects in order for women to make informed choices. The advance of reproductive technology is on the medical horizon. Though new reproductive technologies in Ontario have enabled the births of 207 babies, the costs and risks pale in comparison to the 240,000 childless couples in Canada (Clarke, 1990).

A Future Trend

Reproductive technology is not a trend of the future but is established now and is launching forward at an incredible rate. Such technologies include artificial insemination, embryo transfer, in-vitro fertilization and related technologies like sex determination and surrogate motherhood. The side effects of reproductive technologies bode significant and potentially destructive implications for women. Gena Corea, author of the revealing book *The Mother Machine*, brings these implications to light. She moves the practice of reproductive technologies away from the protective guise of "kindly helping infertile women to have babies" and says that:

> The harm women have been subjected to through DES, the Pill, IUDs, estrogen replacement therapy, tranquillizers, unnecessary hysterectomies and Caesarian sections, etc., has been catalogued. But all this seems to be forgotten when commentators discuss the new reproductive technologies. It is as if the "old" reproductive technologies (such as the IUD) and the "new" ones arose out of two separate medical systems, one of which has a clear record of having hurt women, another of which will help women. But in fact there is one system and one low valuation of women in it (Corea, 1985, p.3).

The problems of surrogate motherhood are already clear. Contracts and financial payments are no guarantee over the strength of emotional attachments or bonds mothers have with their babies. In-vitro fertilization is also a demanding and sometimes relentless process that does not take the well-being of women into account. Women, who must interrupt their lives sometimes for years, are encouraged to try and try again a procedure that offers little hope — a 20 per cent success rate, or rather an 80 per cent failure rate. Women sign a contract that basically signs their bodies over to the specialist. They are not informed of the inherent risks of in-vitro fertilization or made aware that, in many respects, it is not only in its infancy but still in a stage of experimentation. Being prescribed drugs, egg harvesting, implanting and waiting are very physically painful and emotionally wrought experiences. Yet throughout the procedure, doctors speak in technical language referring to the woman's reproductive capacity more or less as a machine. Gena Corea notes that the sole purpose for women has historically been defined by her reproductive function. She has been described as "breeding machines for men," or "defective, yet having one purpose — reproduction." Note that reproduction is a metaphor of the factory and would further suggest that women produce "a marketable product or unit," as artificially inseminated cows are described. Can a woman have dignity in remaining childless? It would seem that the industry of reproductive technology presumes she cannot.

Corea suggests that such technology is aligned with genetic planning, or eugenics, that suggests the goals of selective breeding exist only for fit (open to definition) infertile women who are encouraged to continue using methods of artificial insemination and in-vitro fertilization. Top scientists, aligned with government policy, continue to advocate and develop embryo transfer, cloning (which has recently been perfected) and artificial wombs. Infertile or not, an underlying belief by the powers that be is that women only have the right to have babies if they are the right colour, right class, married and in an underpopulated nation desirous of workers.

Reproductive technologies did not solely progress because leading scientists want infertile women to be blessed with children. Rather, it is believed that children are not an individual matter but a matter for the state. If governments and "experts" cared about individual women's infertility there would be money spent on researching the causes of increasing infertility. Abuse of sterilization is known to go on in the U.S. aimed specifically at poor, minority women. President Clinton is now suggesting single welfare mothers receive no more money for any other children born since the mother became a welfare recipient. In a 1974 report in *January's Family Planning Digest*, 94 per cent of physicians supported sterilization of welfare mothers after their third child. In contrast, pharmacrats loudly cite the right of women to have babies in justifying IVF programs.

The worst science fiction scenario, where the population is sterile and embryos are selectively implanted, is a possibility right now. In fact with cloning, men no longer need to even harvest female eggs. This is a scary thought considering that throughout history up until 1861 men believed they handed over complete babies (their sperm) to women's uteruses that acted simply as temporary houses. Obstetricians and gynaecologists dominated the birthing process in an effort to control the quality of the product (their word) or baby. Doctors have displayed ample disregard for the feelings and well-being of women, if not misogynist tendencies. Boasting of numbers of ovaries collected and performing unnecessarily hostile mutilations in breast removal are some examples. But most interesting is the theory of womb envy that Freud wrote alongside his theories on "penis envy" (Corea, 1985). Though the world has widely heard of Freud's assumption that women experience penis envy, that men may experience "womb envy" has been repressed. Freud also talks of breast envy. In historical metaphors men have longed to see themselves as creators of life and masters of their own familial dynasty or lineage. Finally, men don't need women to conceive babies. They can always buy or borrow a womb for a price. Reproductive technology has become big business, still largely failing in results, that is in search of consumers (the right ones), where the well-being of patients is not a priority. Unfortunately, women professionals in this field continue to be under-involved. One is left to wonder about the direction and future impact of this new technology.

Implications for Social Workers in Health Care Settings

Health care settings provide the largest single field of practice for social workers today (Taylor and Holosko, 1989). The likelihood of social workers meeting sexism in the health care setting is great, if not unavoidable. The hierarchical system of medicine in Canada continues to laud the white male authority of the doctor at the pinnacle of the pyramid. Nursing has become a female job ghetto where women are support staff doing 90 per cent of the work in carrying out the doctors orders yet are low paid in comparison. Social workers have to work in this hierarchical, authoritative structure where nurses also validate the doctor's authority and may resent a meddling, middle-powered social worker. Regardless, social workers need to do all they can to promote a more democratic means of problem-solving — firstly by including the patient in the process.

Information is power, and patients who are kept in the dark by a condescending, patriarchal authority figure have no feeling of control, never mind an ability to make decisions or begin the process of acceptance if necessary. An important role for social workers in helping female patients is to provide them with as much information as possible about the procedures and consequences of their surgeries and medications.

History suggests that their concerns and questions have gone unaddressed, and that male doctors feel they have rights of access to women's bodies with little regard for their feelings or need for dignity, and they may even treat them like children. Social workers in health care settings can speak to patients in nontechnical language when explaining their medical procedures to reduce feelings of inferiority and alienation and to empower them. Many women forego important internal exams because of extreme feelings of embarrassment, feelings which are traditionally shamed and dismissed. Social workers can validate such feelings and even encourage the option of a female doctor where possible if this would alleviate feelings of vulnerability and embarrassment.

Women have long felt that they have relinquished power over their own bodies to patronizing male doctors. For example, one illustration indicates that doctors felt that women should not have any voice in deciding how much of their breast was to be removed, or if it was necessary to remove the whole breast, as women were uninformed and unable to contribute sound input to such decisions.

Women who are still socialized into passive roles need to be included as much as possible in medical decisions that are going to directly affect their bodies and in some cases the quality of their lives. When women are in the hospital about to face surgery, they need solid reassurance based on factual information and respect, not a pat on the head.

As history evidences, women's complaints are more likely to be pathologicalized than men's, who are considered to be more stoic and descriptive of their symptoms. Social workers need to impress upon doctors that their female patient's symptoms are legitimate and deserving of appropriate attention. Social workers need to watch for unnecessary prescribing of addictive tranquillizers to resolve undiagnosed problems that may be more symptomatic of a social or emotional nature — or undiagnosed medical conditions!

Social workers need to guard against unnecessary medical procedures and outline other options to women — especially regarding hysterectomies, estrogen treatments and reproductive technologies. Some medical procedures, like the relentless demands imposed by IVF, do not take the woman's well-being into account. She is regarded as a solely biological unit and her whole person is ignored. Social workers in medical settings need to address the whole person. However, a patient is not likely to meet a social worker in such a setting. Is this a concern to social workers, especially as alternative clinics pop up, that social workers are only to be found in hospitals?

Though Canada has equal access to health care regardless of socioeconomic background, bias against the poor or minorities is evidenced in the decisions made by doctors and administrators, for example, in transplants. The rich are still more worthy of the "best" medical treatment, and social workers may need to advocate on behalf of the politically weak including poor, elderly or minority female clients who are given the brush off. Often assigned as discharge planners, or working in nursing homes or various other agencies, social workers come into contact with elderly patients. Single elderly women in Canada represent a large percentage of Canada's poor and make up the majority of residents in nursing homes. Social workers in health care settings need to be sensitive to their clients' economic, cultural and educational backgrounds, as individual differences and needs beyond physical health concerns are not likely to be addressed by other hospital workers.

The plight of the female physician also needs to be considered. A recent study, *The Feminization of Canadian Medicine: Implications for Health Care Delivery*, points the finger to the "feminization of Canadian medicine" as the root cause for an impending shortage of health care services into the 1990s. The authors of the report, sponsored by the Social Sciences and Humanities Research Council of Canada, establish that female physicians see fewer patients overall, use fewer services and work less hours. The authors infer that female doctors may have less time available due to their family responsibilities. Such studies pave the way to again barring women from entering medical schools. Facts that could suggest female doctors spend more time per patient, don't utilize services unnecessarily and don't maximize patient visits unnecessarily are perhaps more easily interpreted in a negative light, the message being that Canadian society can't afford to "feminize" health care delivery. Social workers also need to support nurses who have made every attempt to professionalize their position, for example with university education and unionization, but who remain in an extremely demanding yet limited role.

Social workers also need to be aware of the changing roles of women and the increasing levels of stress that the average woman faces. Women today are better educated, live alone more of their adult lives and participate in the labour force more consistently than their mothers did. "The New Woman, a product of the rise of women as primary individuals, contrasts sharply with past generations of women, who organized their lives and goals around their family's objectives (Woods et al., 1993, p.392). Increased levels of education and personal resources tend to decrease stress and positively influence women's access to social and health resources (Woods, 1993).

Summary

Sexism in the Canadian health care setting is obvious and rampant today. It is strongly rooted and documented in the sociomedical history of women in western culture. Indeed, devaluation of the female sex is common in most cultures, sometimes in blatant forms (consider the current practice of female infanticide in China and India and the rise of sex determination clinics in Buffalo), and women are bound to internalize such predominant myths and stereotypes perpetuated by those in authority.

Positively, changes in the medical profession are evident, especially since the rise of the women's health movement. Statistics show more and more women are entering Canadian medical schools. In the 1990/91 school year 44.4 per cent of the total enrolment in Canadian faculties of medicing were female compared to only seven per cent in 1957/58 and just under 18 per cent in 1970/71 (Bolaria and Dickinson, 1991, pp. 164-166). The influx of women into medical schools was hoped by some to bring traditionally feminine qualities to the profession such as sensitivity, compassion and nurturance. Such, however, has not been the case.

Generally, entrants into medical education are steeped in a background of science and mathematics. The university curricula and standards are largely uniform and, using the regurgitation of facts as the focal learning tool, tend to ultimately have a homogenizing effect on students. First year female medical students are shown to value the human, social and preventative aspects of patient care more than their male contemporaries, but by graduation there are few differenced (Maheux, et al., 1988). The socialization effect of medical education produces both male and female physicians who display comparable diagnostic and therapeutic skills and common knowledge bases. Some have noted that "women physicians more nearly resemble men physicians in professional attributes than they do other women in the population" (Kirk, 1994, p. 176). Further, both male and female physicians largely carry the same sexist and paternalistic theories about women's health into medical practice.

Early on in the educational process female students who do complain about sexist jokes or harassment are considered troublemakers and are often not supported by their female peers (Kirk, 1994). In one study 34 per cent of female students experienced gender discrimination and 62 per cent observed other female students who had experienced gender discrimination (Grant, 1988).

There are also few female role models for medical students. Only 5-20 per cent of the instructors in medical schools are women. And few women are in powerful professional positions. Women are tracked early on into certain specialities, such as pediatrics and family medicine, and are discouraged from entering others. In particular, surgery has remained "the old boys club" where women are not considered to have the physical stamina or emotional stability to handle the job. Women entering surgery today find few female colleagues, no maternity leaves, no separate change rooms and inflexible timetables.

Women physicians are accused of working fewer hours than their male colleagues. Women do work 90 per cent of the hours that men do. However, they continue to be torn by their family responsibilities. One study revealed that in dual-doctor marriages, 19 out of 21 wives reported compromising their careers due to their marriages, and all of them reported their husband's careers were given priority (Johnson, et al., 1991).

It is no wonder given the competitive and homogenizing nature of the medical educational process in Canadian universities, plus the pausity of female role models as instructors or leaders and the lack of support from female colleagues in fighting sexism, that little change has occurred to date. However, women doctors are beginning to become commonplace in the profession. At the same time, social workers who are not educated in the strict medical model where the body is viewed as a quasi-machine, have a distinct advantage over physicians. They can exert external pressure by promoting the patient as a whole person and not merely a collection of body parts. This promotes the concept that the role of the patient in their own healing process is an important addition to the role of the physician. Social workers can strengthen the patient's role in their healing process while working in conjunction with medical intervention.

As women, we are obliged to learn about our own bodies so we can better represent ourselves in medical decisions that affect us directly. As social workers we need to support female physicians and nurses and encourage their male colleagues to find it worth their while to eliminate sexism. Involvement in the enacting of more protective legislative policy is integral — i.e., demand greater testing of new medicines and devices. As professionals, social workers need to be more involved in the decision-making processes both at the micro and macro levels. To date, the study of sexism in medical settings strongly reflects a feminist perspective. This view needs to broaden to include all people. Being aware of the role of the female patient in a historical perspective makes clearer today's stereotypes and expectations placed on women. Although great strides have been taken since the women's health movement, the medical system is still functioning within a patriarchal hierarchy. Women are still easily considered neurotic patients or inferior employees and may be treated in a condescending and manipulative manner.

The implications for social workers in health care settings are numerous. They can help to turn a dehumanizing technical process into a more humane one by paying attention to the ignored aspects of the whole person — their feelings, needs, fears, hopes and concerns. With a unique knowledge base, quite different from their medically trained co-workers, social workers can play a vital and supportive role by empowering their clients and by not contributing to the hierarchy where doctors are gods and all others facilitators of their orders.

Endnote:

[1]   The *New York Times* reported in July 1974 that a female intern at the University of Michigan was not allowed to be present during an exam because a man's genitals would be exposed.

References

Abbott, A. 1994. "A Feminist Approach to Substance Abuse Treatment and Service Delivery." *Social Work in Health Care*. 19: 3/4, 67-83.

Bolaria, B.S. and Dickinson, H.D. (eds.). 1994. *Health, Illness, and Health Care in Canada*, second edition. Toronto: Harcourt Brace.

Bullough, V. and Voght, M. 1984. "Women, Menstruation, and Nineteenth-Century Medicine." Leavitt, Judith (ed.), *Women and Health in America*. Madison: University of Wisconsin Press.

Clarke, J. N. 1990. *Health, Illness and Medicine in Canada*. Toronto: McClelland and Stewart.

Corea, G. 1977. *The Hidden Malpractice: How American Medicine Treats Women as Patients and Professionals*. New York: William Morrow and Company.

Corea, G. 1985. *The Mother Machine: Reproductive Technologies from Artificial Insemination to Artificial Wombs*. New York: Harper and Row.

Ehrenreich, B. and English, D. 1979. *For Her Own Good: 150 Years of the Experts' Advice to Women*. New York: Anchor Books.

Giacomini, M. et al. 1986. "Gender Bias in Human Anatomy Textbook Illustrations." *Psychology of Women Quarterly*. 10: 413-420.

Gilman, C. P. 1993. "The Yellow Wallpaper [1892]," in Barnet, S., M. Berman and W. Burto (eds.), *An Introduction to Literature*, 10th edition. New York: Harper Collins.

Grant, L. 1988. "The Gender Climate of Medical School: Perspectives of Women and Men Students." *The Journal of the American Medical Association*, 43:4, 109-119.

Hubbard, R. 1990. *The Politics of Women's Biology*. New Brunswick: Rutgers University Press.

Johnson, C., Johnson, B. and Liese, B. 1991. "Dual-Doctor Marriages: The British Experience." *The Journal of the American Medical Association*, 46:5, 155-163.

Kirk, J. 1994. "A Feminist Analysis of Women in Medical Schools," in Bolaria, B.S. and H.D. Dickinson (eds.), *Health, Illness, and Health Care in Canada*, second edition. Toronto: Harcourt Brace.

Kurz, D. 1987. "Emergency Department Responses to Battered Women: Resistance to Medicalization." *Social Problems*. 34: 1, 69-80.

Mackie, M. 1991. *Gender Relations in Canada: Further Explorations*. Toronto: Butterworths.

Maheux, B., Dufort, F. and Beland, F. 1988. "Professional and Sociopolitical Attitudes of Medical Students: Gender Differences Reconsidered." *The Journal of the American Medical Association*, 43:3, 73-75.

Mitchinson, W. and McGinnis, J. D. (eds.). 1988. *Essays in the History of Canadian Medicine*. Toronto: McClelland and Stewart.

Olson, M. 1994. "Reclaiming the 'Other:' Women, Health Care and Social Work." *Social Work in Health Care*, 19: 3/4, 1-16.

Ruzek, S. B. 1978. *The Women's Health Movement: Feminist Alternatives to Medical Control*. New York: Praeger.

Strong-Boag, V.. 1981. "Canada's Women Doctors: Feminism Constrained," in Shortt, S. (ed.), *Medicine in Canadian Society: Historical Perspectives*. Montreal: McGill-Queens University Press.

Taylor, P. and Holosko, M. 1989. *Social Work Practice in Health Care Settings*. Toronto: Canadian Scholars' Press.

Web, C. (ed.). 1986. *Feminist Practice in Health Care.* Chichester: John Wiley and Sons.

Wetzel, J. W. 1994. "Depression: Women at Risk." *Social Work in Health Care*, 19: 3/4, 85-108.

Williams, A. P., Domnick-Pierre, K. and Vayda, E. 1990. *The Feminization of Canadian Medicine: Implications for Health Care Delivery.* Toronto: Institute for Social Research, York University.

Woods, N. F. et al. 1993. *The New Woman: Health-Promoting and Health Damaging Behaviors.* Health Care for Women International. 14: 389-405.

Chapter III
The Religious Roots of Women's Inequality

Pamela Milne

The focus of this chapter will be on the role that religion has played historically in constructing our ideas about the nature of woman and the social relationships between women and men. These ideas are still embedded in the fabric of everyday lives. The consequences of thinking about women, which have emanated from religious institutions over the centuries, have had a profoundly negative and limiting impact on virtually every woman's life whether she regards herself as religious or not. Religious gender ideology is also at the root of the traditional notions of family in Canadian society. Opposition to unmarried mothers or to the notion of gay and lesbian families frequently arises from the religious right who understand the Bible or some other religious text to condemn such arrangements.

The issue of religion is, therefore, relevant both to the woman social worker whose own life and world view has been influenced by religious teaching about women and gender relations, and to the social worker who works with women whose life experiences and crises will have been affected, either directly or indirectly, by religious values. Beyond this, however, it is important for the social worker today to be aware of, and sensitive to, the fact that Canada is no longer the "Christian" country it used to be. Christianity may still be regarded as normative insofar as the Christian calendar and Christian festivals still structure our society. But the reality now is that, as the Canadian population has become racially and culturally diverse, there has been a steady increase in the visibility and centrality of religions such as Islam, Buddhism, Hinduism, Sikhism and New Age Spiritualities. People who practice religions other than Christianity now expect their religious traditions to be accorded the same respect and societal privileges accorded Christianity. Hence, the social worker of today must become more attuned to religious issues.

Introduction

Canadian society is largely secular, and religion, which once played a major role in politics and the workplace, seems now to be a private matter. However, despite the seeming secularity of Canadian society today, religion remains an important factor that has shaped and continues to reshape our everyday lives. Not even the most ardent secularist is unaffected by religion. Many of our national legal holidays, for example, are basically religious holidays, even if most Canadians do not observe them religiously (Christmas, Good Friday and Easter). There are, however, many other, more subtle ways in which religion continues to have an impact on the lives of virtually all Canadians.

The goal of this chapter is to examine how women have generally been portrayed by religion and how these portrayals have influenced women's lives. Ideally, each of the major eastern and western religions should be considered individually, but such a task is too large for the present context. It can be said that all the major religions are male religions, insofar as they focus on a male-imaged deity, have sacred texts which are primarily male-authored and interpreted and have been structurally organized in ways that are more beneficial to men than to women. Consequently, none has functioned to promote full equality and independence for women (Carmody, 1989, p. 3).

A dominant function of all major religions over the centuries has been to justify the restriction of women's lives and the subordination of women to men. Therefore, examples from the three western world religions, Judaism, Christianity and Islam, will be examined to illustrate the negative impact of religion on women's lives. To the extent that Canadian social structures have been influenced more by Christianity to date, Christian constructions of woman will be discussed in more detail.

Patriarchy

Canadian society remains fundamentally patriarchal. Patriarchy may be described as "a system of male authority which oppresses women through its social, political and economic institutions" (Humm, 1989, p. 159), or as "a sexual system of power in which the male possesses superior power and economic privilege" (Eisenstein, 1979, p. 17). A patriarchal society is one in which men fill most decision-making positions, have preferential access to education and control most of the capital. It is one in which sex roles tend to be stereotyped. Men are thought to be better suited for some activities and functions while women are deemed better suited for others. For example, men should be breadwinners while women should be homemakers. Another feature of a patriarchy is that the work men do is valued more highly and given greater financial compensation than women's work.

Canadian society, despite the legal equality accorded women in the Charter of Rights and Freedoms, is still one in which women have less freedom of choice of profession, less access to higher education, less access to well-paid jobs and less access to justice and the legal system. There is a deeply ingrained societal attitude that women are inferior to men. Because of the assumed superiority of men, it has been deemed appropriate in most societies, including Canada until very recently, for men to dominate women and for women to be subordinate to men. There are many ways in which this attitude is manifested, but one that is relatively new to the Canadian scene is that of sex selection in pregnancy. The belief that males are more desirable than females leads some to abort pregnancies if the foetus is female. In some parts of the world where the technology is not available to determine the sex of the foetus, female babies are allowed to die or are killed if the family already has one or more girls and no boys. Such actions represent the extreme end of a continuum of violence toward women, which is rooted in centuries of religiously sanctioned belief that women are inferior forms of the human species.

Feminism and Feminist Analysis of Religion

The feminist movement of the twentieth century has brought about the first sustained challenge to the type of thinking that values males over females. Because religion has played such a key role in promoting the idea of women's inferiority, feminists have been engaged in the critical analysis of religious systems and teachings. The work of feminist scholars of religion is important because, until very recently, women were generally excluded from the formal study of religion.

Many women today avoid the terms "feminism" and "feminist." As women have made gains toward equality, there has been a growing effort to resist and suppress this movement. One strategy in this resistance movement has been to link feminism with a host of negative ideas. Women who internalize this negative view are inclined to say, "I'm not a feminist, but I believe in equality for women." It is important, however, to reclaim the word "feminism" and to use it in the positive sense in which it was coined. There is no one standard definition of feminism, but a survey of feminist writings reveals that, for most feminists, feminism has as its goal the implementation of full equality — legal, social, political, economic and religious — between women and men.

The feminist study of religion has provided us with remarkable insights into the relationship between religious teaching and the oppression of women in society. In the remainder of this chapter, some feminist insights as they relate to the three western world religions will be described.

The Image of Woman in Sacred Texts

Women today find themselves defined and constrained by ideas about women created many hundreds of years ago in very different cultural settings. Judaism, Christianity and Islam are often called religions of the book because they have written texts that they hold to be inspired by god and, therefore, the authoritative, or foundational, documents of the religion. In Judaism, the sacred text is the Tanak. It contains material written between about 1200-165 b.c.e. Christians also regard the Tanak as sacred, but they call it the Old Testament and add to it a collection of texts called the New Testament. The New Testament, which deals with the life, ministry and death of Jesus and the early decades of the Christian church, took shape between about 50-125 c.e. The word "bible" is generally used to refer to these Jewish and Christian scriptures. In Islam, the Qur'an is the most authoritative scripture. Muslims believe that the Jewish and Christian scriptures are genuine revelations from god, but that the last and definitive revelations are those made to the prophet Muhammad between 610-632 c.e.

All of these sacred traditions are ancient and, because they are sacred texts, they can not be added to or subtracted from. Their canon, or collection, is fixed. This is one source of problems women face in these religions. While some problematic aspects of the biblical tradition have been deemed not to represent the divine intention by most Jews and Christians, others are still retained. Slavery, for example, was simply an accepted social institution in the biblical world and is never condemned in the Bible. Today, most people would read the texts on slavery as merely descriptions of an existing social situation, not as prescriptions for how we should act today. But when it comes to the Bible's comments on women, many more people regard them as prescribing proper behaviour and relationships for our present society. For this reason, it is crucial to look at what such sacred texts say about women and reflect on how these texts continue to influence our world.

Women as the Property of Men

The most fundamental idea about women contained in the Bible is that women are property belonging to men. A woman begins her life as her father's property and eventually becomes her husband's property. In some instances, when her father or husband dies, a woman can become her brother's property. Thus, the concept of woman-as-man's-property is basic to understanding all other aspects of family relations and codes of sexual conduct.

The clearest illustration of women's status as property is found within the Decalogue or Ten Commandments in Exodus 20 and Deuteronomy 5. The first point to note is that these commandments are only addressed to men. The "you" in the commandment is a masculine grammatical form in the original Hebrew. The exclusion of women becomes clear even in English in the last commandment, which reads: "You shall not covet your neighbour's house; you shall not covet your neighbour's wife, or male or female slave, or ox, or donkey, or anything that belongs to your neighbour" (Exodus 20: 17; cf. Deuteronomy 5:21). A man owns his wife as he owns his land, buildings, slaves and animals. Because a wife is considered a man's possession, she may be disposed of in a way analogous to his other property. For that reason, according to biblical law, a man may divorce his wife but a wife is not able to divorce her husband (Deuteronomy 24:1). By the time of Jesus, this divorce text was interpreted so liberally by some, that a woman could be divorced for any trivial action that displeased her husband, even burning dinner. As a counter to such attitudes, Jesus seems to have gone to the opposite extreme, insisting that in marriage husband and wife are joined together by God and no man can dissolve this bond (Matthew 19:1-9). While this solution may have given economic protection to wives who, if divorced, were likely to join the ranks of the very poor, it was not an ideal solution for wives who found themselves in abusive relationships. A father was allowed to sell his daughter as a slave (Exodus 21:7) or sacrifice his daughter in payment for a religious vow (Judges 11). Men could take women captives in war and make them wives (Deuteronomy 21:11-13). Men could have several wives at the same time but a woman was allowed only one husband. Furthermore, because women were themselves considered as property, they normally could not own or inherit property. Only if a man died without leaving sons could daughters inherit (Numbers 27:1-11), but in such cases daughters were required to marry within the father's tribe so that the property stayed with the male kinship line (Numbers 36:1-12).

There is a clear sexual double standard in the Bible. Women are regarded as the property of men; a woman's sexuality belongs not to her but to her husband, father or brother. Men are free to be sexually active with few restrictions, but women are highly restricted. So, for example, there is no prohibition or social stigma attached to a man who uses the services of a prostitute (Genesis 38; 1 Kings 1; Leviticus 21:9). A woman was required to be a virgin at marriage and could be required to prove it, but a man was not. Failure to prove virginity could result in a young woman being stoned or burned to death (Deuteronomy 22:13-21; Leviticus 21:13-14).

The concept of rape does not exist in the Bible. A man may have sex forcibly with any woman who is available to him so long as she is not another man's wife. In Judges 19, for example, a priest turns his concubine over to the men of Gibeah who gang-rape her all night. The priest is indignant, not because they have raped his concubine but because they threatened him with sexual assault. In a similar story in Genesis 19, Lot offers his two daughters to the townsmen in a similar circumstance. Both stories illustrate that while it is not acceptable for men to sexually assault other men, it is quite acceptable for men to sexually assault women.

If a man has sexual intercourse with an unmarried woman, his only penalty is that he must pay the bride price, that he marry the woman, if her father is willing, and that he may not divorce her (Deuteronomy 22:28-29; Exodus 34). The only women who are sexually off limits are married women. Sex with a married woman (the marital status of the man is of no consequence) is adultery. Adultery and incest (between a son and his father's wife) are serious offences ranking with murder (Exodus 20:14; Deuteronomy 5:18). If caught, both parties are put to death (Leviticus 20:10-11). This is a serious crime, not as a sexual transgression but as a property transgression. The violation of another man's sexual property is an enormous blow to his honour and thus must be appropriately avenged.

Like the Bible, the Qur'an also sets out legal restrictions on women's lives that differ from those placed on men. As in the Bible, the word "you" implies a male audience. The revelation in the Qur'an is conceived as revelation to men, which occasionally talks about women. Surah (chapter 4) is entitled "Women" and contains many, but not all, of the teachings about women.

When women are discussed in the Qur'an it is usually in the context of marriage, divorce, inheritance and modesty (Smith, 1987). A Muslim man is allowed to marry up to four women, if he is able to provide for all equally. This qualification has meant that historically a relatively small percentage of Muslim men have been able to afford more than two wives. The women a man marries may be Muslim, but they do not have to be Muslim (Surah 4:3). In theory, a woman has the legal right to refuse to marry a particular man and to negotiate a marriage contract with terms that give her certain securities. In practice, many women were and are unaware of this right or unable to access it. Historically, fathers have often arranged marriages when daughters were very young. A Muslim woman, on the other hand, may be married to only one man and he must be a Muslim.

While it is technically possible for a wife to divorce her husband, divorce is usually the prerogative of the husband (Surah 4:24). Traditionally, custody of the children goes to fathers once the children are between the ages of seven and puberty. The Qur'an accords women greater inheritance rights than does the Bible. Women are legally permitted to inherit and own property, but they are entitled to inherit a portion that is only half as much as a male heir inherits (Surah 4:11-12).

As with the biblical tradition, the Qur'an treats women's sexuality as the property of men. Adultery, therefore, is a serious offence except in cases where the married woman is a captive from war. Incest, sex with women who belong to men who are closely related, is also forbidden (Surah 4:26). Women are required not to expose themselves immodestly to those who are not family members (Surah 24:31). Women must veil themselves to ensure modesty (Surah 33:55-59).

Women as a Danger to Men

In both the biblical and Qur'anic traditions women, particularly women's sexuality, is thought to pose a danger to men. Principally, this is a danger to men's honour. Protecting men's honour often means making sure that their women are securely under their control. The veiling of women as prescribed in the Qur'an and the practice of secluding women, or restricting them from contact with men to whom they are not related, are practices that arose as ways to reduce the danger women posed to men's honour. Women who are unattached to a man or not adequately controlled by a man are seen as especially problematic.

The Bible is filled with warnings about "loose women." Proverbs 1-9 consist of the counsel a father gives to his son on surviving in the world. Repeatedly, the son is advised to follow Lady Wisdom and the avoid the Foreign Woman (or Lady Folly). While these terms are used metaphorically, the foolish woman bears a striking resemblance to ordinary women. The son is warned that the speech of the two women sounds very similar and thus it is difficult to distinguish the message of one from the other (Yee, 1989). If the son chooses Wisdom, he will find life, but if he chooses Folly, he will find death (Proverbs 2:5). The father warns about the loose woman who will sexually seduce the son.

Texts such as these give evidence of and support for an environment in which women's bodies and words are deemed dangerous not just to a man's honour but to his very life. They create the need to silence women's voices and to control women's bodies. In New Testament texts from the period of the early church, women, who earlier had played a central and vocal role in the ministry of Jesus, are instructed to dress modestly, learn silently and be submissive to men (1 Timothy 2:8-12).

Women as Inferior and Subordinate to Men

Closely related to the concepts that women are the property of men and constitute a danger to men is the notion that women are inferior to men and therefore must be subordinate to men. In the Bible, marriage is frequently used as a metaphor for the relationship between God and Israel. God is imaged as a faithful husband, while Israel is imaged as a faithless or promiscuous wife. Hosea 1-3 actually uses the prophet's own marriage to Gomer as a model. While this imagery initially appears to function well in giving readers a sense that the relationship between God and the people is as intimate as that between a husband and wife, it also serves to give another message that emphasizes the inferiority of women and the right of a husband to dominate or "lord it over" his wife. By saying that the divine-human relationship is like a marriage, this metaphor also says that a marriage is a hierarchical power relationship. God and Israel are not equals: the divine is obviously superior to the human. So marriage is only a useful metaphor if readers also assume that husbands are to God as wives are to Israel. In other words, husbands are superior to wives as God is superior to Israel and husbands are lords over their wives as God is Lord over Israel. Metaphors always read in both directions; as Mary Daly has observed, when male is God, God is male (Daly, 1973, p. 19). The metaphorical link between God and man in the marriage metaphor reinforces the strongly male-imaged deity found throughout the entire Bible.

In the New Testament there are a series of passages, collectively known as the Household Codes, which give a new formulation to the hierarchized model of family (Balch, 1981). Ephasians 5:21-6:4; Colossians 3:18-4:1; and 1 Peter 3:1-6 are among the passages that enlist the idea of the patriarchal household, borrowed from the Graeco-Roman world, as a model for the social and religious structure of the emerging Christian community. Whereas in the earlier Jesus movement the commitment had been to radical equality between men and women, Jews and Gentiles, slaves and free men (Galatians 3:28), the Christian community of the early second century abandoned this vision of equality and reclaimed the hierarchy of the status quo in which wives were subordinate to husbands, children to their parents and slaves to their masters. These texts create the paradigms husband/parent/master and wife/child/slave. The members of the latter paradigm qualify as property of the first.

The biblical text most often cited as evidence for women's inferiority, however, is Genesis 2-3, the story of Adam and Eve. There is much debate among feminist scholars about whether this story was written to justify male domination of women or as a condemnation of that domination. Whatever its original purpose, it seems clear that the story was used by later biblical writers and others in the Jewish, Christian and Muslim traditions to demonstrate the inferiority of women. In this later reading of the story it is claimed that woman is secondary to man because Eve was formed after Adam and from a rib of Adam. Being second is taken to imply inferiority. Moreover, these traditions blame Eve for the transgression of the divine command not to eat the fruit of one of the trees in the Garden of Eden. Had Eve not "tempted" Adam, he would not have disobeyed. Eve is taken as the paradigm or model of all women who, like Eve, suffer the punishment of pain in childbirth and subordination to man for their role in bringing sin and death into the world. In the Christian scripture, the idea of woman as responsible for sin can be seen in 2 Corinthians 11:3 and 1 Timothy 3:14. The latter text makes the clearest statement that women's subordinate status is a consequence of the actions of Eve. In the Islamic tradition the Adam and Eve story is not discussed in the Qur'an but is taken up and used in the Hadith, sayings attributed to Muhammad. Despite the fact that the Qur'an claims that man and woman were created from a single soul (Surah 4:1), Islamic theology of woman has been defined on the basis of the less authoritative Hadith. Six *ahadith* describing women as having been created from the bent rib of man have been particularly important in the development of the belief among Muslims that women are secondary to men, responsible for the fall of man and thus created for man (Hassan).

The Qur'an is not, however, without problems for women. Surah 2:228 claims that men are a step or degree above women while Surah 4:34 maintains that men are in charge of women because God has given preference to men over women. Men, therefore, must provide support for women while women must be obedient to men (Smith, 1987, p. 236; Carmody, 1989, p. 193).

Religion as a Liberating and Oppressing Force for Women

In the foregoing survey of scriptural texts, the focus has been on the negative depiction of women. This, however, does not tell the whole story. Characteristic of many new religious movements, including the Moses movement, which became the Israelite and then Jewish religions, the Jesus movement, which became Christianity, and the Muhammad movement, which became Islam, there was a brief period during the founding years when women appear to have been accorded a higher status than they had previously had in society. Although most evidence of these times has been lost, it is possible to recover fragmentary evidence.

In the time between Moses and David, when Israel was a religious confederacy (ca. 1200-1000 b.c.e.), we find references to women like Miriam and Deborah. Later, both women were portrayed as prophets since this was the only public religious role still open to women. Inferred in these later references are images of women who were independent leaders in their own right. Miriam is remembered in at least one text as a co-leader with her brothers Moses and Aron (Micah 6:4), while Deborah seems to have functioned as a deliverer in a manner similar to the men who played this role, e.g., Gideon, Samuel, Othniel, etc. The earliest tradition gives her the title "mother in Israel" even though she is never said to have had children (Judges 5:7). This seems to be a title of honour and leadership. In later times, Deborah's place in history is usurped by her cowardly general, Barak (1 Samuel 12:11; Hebrews 11:32).

During the period of the monarchy, from David to the fall of Jerusalem in 587 b.c.e., women's roles were restricted largely to the domestic sphere. A woman's role was to be a wife and to provide her husband with male offspring. Occasionally, we glimpse women like the prophet Huldah (Jeremiah's aunt), but she, too, was a wife in addition to being a prophet (2 Kings 22:14-20).

In the centuries between the fall of Jerusalem and the rise of the Jesus movement there is evidence of a growing misogyny (hatred of women) and gynophobia (fear of women). Many of the biblical texts discussed above arise in this period (Proverbs 1-9). Other writings from this period that did not find their way into the Jewish collection of scripture, but which were used as scripture by the early Christian church, such as the book of Sirach, give chillingly hostile portrayals of women: "An iniquity is small compared to a woman's iniquity" (Sirach 25:19); "From a woman sin had its beginning, and because of her we all die" (Sirach 25:24); "A bad wife is a chafing yoke; taking hold of her is like grasping a scorpion" (Sirach 26:7).

Women seemed to have played a central role in the life and ministry of Jesus. In fact, it is possible to argue that a woman, Mary Magdalene, was the most important disciple of Jesus. The Gospels depict her as a travelling disciple like some of the men (Luke 8:1-3) and as one of a small group who stayed with Jesus as he was crucified (Mark 15:40-41; Matthew 27:55-56; Luke 23:49; John 19:25). She is said to have been the first person to discover the tomb of Jesus empty (Mark 161; Matthew 28:1; Luke 24:10; John 20:1) and, in some Gospels, she is the first person to whom the risen Christ is said to have appeared (Matthew 28:9-10; John 20:11-18). Hence she may be regarded as the first apostle. Indeed, it appears that the beginning of the Christian tradition depends heavily on the witness of a woman. So central was Mary Magdalene to the early Jesus movement that she seems to have become a major problem to the later church as it moved toward adopting patriarchal structures. If male leadership was to be the norm, her role had to be undermined. And so we see an effective process of character assassination occurring through the centuries as Mary Magdalene is identified with the unnamed sinner in Luke 7:36-50. Although the New Testament never says or even suggests she is a prostitute, she is, today, almost universally thought of as such. Once her character was sullied in this way it was easy for Peter to replace her as the rock upon which the Christian church was founded. Although the early church used the houses of prominent women for its table fellowship as it carried its missionary activity into the Graeco-Roman world, women were gradually excluded from the leadership roles they once held. The clerical culture that developed in the Christian church was as male as the cultic culture of Judaism.

A similar pattern can be detected in Islam. It seems apparent that Islam would not have had its beginning as a religion had it not been for a woman. Muhammad's first wife, Khadija, was a wealthy merchant who was able to provide Muhammad with the economic support that permitted him time for spiritual reflection. When he first began receiving divine revelations, it was Khadija who gave him the encouragement to accept them. While she was alive, Khadija was Muhammad's only wife. After her death, however, he married eight more times, and whereas no effort seems to have been made to place restrictions on Khadija's activities, veiling and seclusion seem to have been introduced for these other wives. From this point on, the lives of Muslim women became subject to increasing restrictions.

The Development of the Traditions

Apart from their initial stages, the major western religions have functioned more to restrict and oppress than to liberate women. Each of these traditions has regarded the male as the norm and female as abnormal. Women's bodies seem to have fascinated and frightened male religious thinkers.

In the Mishnah, compiled between 200 and 500 c.e., Judaism developed a system of purity laws that defined women as sources of impurity because of their menstrual cycles. A menstruating woman brought ritual pollution to all that she touched. Therefore, a practice of segregating men and women during ritual and of denying women access to religious leadership roles developed in traditional Judaism. Today, this system is still observed in Orthodox and, to some extent, in Conservative Jewish denominations, whereas women are now being ordained as rabbis in Reform and Reconstructionist denominations.

Christianity is characterized by numerous vitriolic, misogynous pronouncements by leading fathers and doctors of the post New Testament church. In general, women were regarded as evil by nature and physically weak, a combination that led them to use seduction to plot against men (Daly, 1968; Ruether, 1974).

Origen, a third century c.e. author, wrote that every soul is stained because it is clothed in a human body, but the soul of a woman is stained by the corruption of a woman's body. He argued that God does not stoop to look at what is feminine and corporeal.

In the fourth century, the anti-woman, anti-body, anti-sex thinking of previous centuries crystallized in the theology of Augustine. Drawing on the philosophy of Plato, Augustine constructed a set of dualisms that firmly entrenched women in the role of "Other." In Augustine's scheme, man is to rational is to the image of God as woman is to body is to irrational is to not-the-image of God. The outcome of this thinking was a positive emphasis on virginity, which kept men sexually apart from the dangers of women's bodies, and a negative emphasis on marriage, which at best was a necessary evil (Daly, 1968, pp. 85-90; Ruether, 1974, pp. 150-183; Clark and Richardson, 1977, pp. 69-77).

The situation for Christian women significantly declined in the thirteenth-century teachings of Thomas Aquinas. Aquinas drew on the biological ideas of Aristotle to argue that women are defective by nature. He taught that the male semen was the active force in procreation while the womb was the passive receptacle in which the male seed grew. If the pregnancy went well, the male seed would emerge from the womb as a male child. But if something went wrong during pregnancy, a defect would occur and the child born would be female. Therefore, by definition in Aquinas's theology, women were defective examples of the human species while men were more perfect examples of the human species.

Women are literally "misbegotten males" who are defective physically, intellectually and morally and thus subordinate to men in every realm (McLaughlin, 1973, p. 218; Daly, 1968, pp. 90-95; Clark and Richardson, 1977, pp. 78-101). Accordingly, women are suitable "helpmates" for man only in procreation. Women cannot receive sacraments like Holy Orders, i.e., they cannot be priests because in their condition of subjection they can not signify "eminence of degree." Christ could only have assumed human form in the male sex because the male sex is more nearly perfect and strong, and thus more suitable for divine expression than the female sex (McLaughlin, 1973, p. 220).

In Europe, in the centuries following the development of Aquinas's theology of woman as defective by nature, a horrific persecution of women, driven largely by the institutional church, unfolded. In 1484, Pope Innocent VIII published a papal document deploring witchcraft. Two years later, two Dominican priests of the same religious order to which Thomas Aquinas had belonged published the *Malleus Maleficarum*, literally the "Hammer against the Female Evildoers," which served as a handbook for inquisitors. This document crystallized all the negative Christian teachings about women in a profoundly disturbing way. Women were depicted as being easy prey for the devil and prone to witchcraft because of their carnal lust. This document deserves serious study as a fundamental example of the way in which male fear and hatred of women can be projected onto women. Hundreds of thousands of women in Europe were executed as witches as a result of this document. It is difficult to think of a more significant example where women have been victimized because of their sex and blamed for their own victimization. These "Burning Times" were a time of holocaust for women (Clark and Richardson, 1977, pp. 116-130).

The Protestant Reformation in the sixteenth century brought some gains for women, such as the rehabilitation of marriage and access to education. Except for a few sectarian movements, however, mainstream Protestantism continued to regard women as suited by nature to motherhood and domestic roles rather than public leadership roles in society and the church. With the Reformation, women gained the role of pastor's wife but lost the role of nun, the only economically viable alternative to marriage for most Christian women (Clark and Richardson, 1977, pp. 131-148; Douglas, 1974, pp. 292-318).

Luther, for example, wrote that men possess intelligence because they have broad shoulders and narrow hips. In contrast, women have broad hips and narrow shoulders, which indicates that they are best suited for sitting upon their fundament keeping house and raising children. Virtually all reformers assume that wives are to be subject to their husbands as set out in the household codes (Douglas, 1974, p. 299). Luther went so far as to argue that witchcraft was not a sin of the flesh but one which arises from female foolishness and mental weakness. Therefore, the best remedy for witchcraft is for women to accept their God-given place as housewives, to accept themselves as inferior creatures and to give their wills over to their husbands (Brauner, 1989, p. 37). Like many male theologians before him, Luther appealed to the Adam and Eve story as explanation for the cause of women's inferior status. He even justifies the practice of a woman taking her husband's name on the basis of this text:

> when a woman marries a man, she loses the name of her family, and is called by the name of husband. It would be unnatural if a husband wanted to be called by his wife's name. This is an indication and a confirmation of the punishment or subjection which a woman incurred through her sin. Likewise, if the husband changes his place of residence, the woman is compelled to follow him as her lord. So manifold are the traces in nature which remind us of sin and of our misfortune. (Clarke and Richardson, 1977, p. 148)

This reference to the practice of a woman taking her husband's name upon marriage and following him as he changes his place of residence brings the discussion back to the contemporary situation in Canada. Today, most women adopt their husband's surnames with little thought to the religious implications of this act. Indeed, this practice is clearly related to the idea that women are the property of men. This concept is also reinforced in traditional Christian wedding ceremonies in which a father "gives" his daughter to another man, the husband. This ceremony is designed as a property exchange. Today, few husbands have to pay a bride price but many fathers expect their sons-in-law to assume economic responsibility for their daughters after marriage. Until the recent family law reforms, women who were divorced usually got little in the way of the assets of the marriage, which were generally regarded as the husband's property. Few realize that women in Canada did not have legal status as persons until as recently as 1929.

Marital problems continue to arise from the belief that men are the head of the household and the breadwinners in the family. Economic realities often make this impossible, and many women have careers that parallel, and occasionally surpass, those of their partners. It is still unusual for a man to give up his job to follow his wife as she progresses in her career. Most women still expect to place their careers outside the home second to those of their husbands. Few, however, realize that the social pressure to conform to this standard is based on religious doctrines that hold women to be inferior because of their responsibility for bringing sin and death into the world. Such beliefs remain a powerful force in maintaining structures of sexual inequality.

To date, major religious systems have not led the way in the struggle for women's equality. Nor has the educational system done much to raise the consciousness of women and men about the underlying religiously inspired values that make the roots of sexism in our culture so difficult to eradicate.

Although religions have had an essentially negative impact on women's lives in Canada, it is also the case that religions have benefited women. Indeed, for some women in our society religion is an important part of their self-identity, and their sense of spirituality is central in allowing them to cope on a daily basis. It is important to make the distinction between one's personal belief system, which may be quite positive and sustaining, and organized or institutional religion. The foregoing survey has focused on how these religious institutions have functioned in sustaining the attitudes toward women that we encounter in today's society.

Women's experience has been excluded from the construction of all major religious systems so that women tend to be objects that are talked about in religious texts and authoritative pronouncements rather than subjects who speak for themselves. The dominant religious images of woman have been male defined. Only now are women within these religions beginning to challenge this situation and to demand the right to image themselves.

Although we are now seeing some changes, men are still generally thought of as better suited for public offices and more competent to hold senior executive positions. Some entire professions remain highly male-dominated. Moreover, the new sexism evident today in efforts to roll back the equity gains women have made often derive from religiously conservative forces that continue to insist that women were created principally for the purpose of procreation and that their proper role is in the home as wives and mothers.

Implications for Social Work

Despite the negative impact of organized religions on women's lives, religious experience has always been an important part of the lives of women. Even when excluded from official structures of mainstream religions, women have often organized their own religious associations peripherally attached to those official structures. It is significant to note that women have often chosen to give expression to their religious commitment by establishing charitable organizations to address the needs of the poor, the sick and children (Prentice, et al., 1988; Mitchinson, 1987). Many hostels, hospitals and schools have their origins in the commitment to social justice of religious women. Historically, some of their organizations may be regarded as the precursors of organized social work.

Considering this background, the challenge for women in social work today becomes one of reconciling traditional religious values within professional feminist social work values. First, the traditional religious values support a hierarchy in the family and society in which women are subordinate to men. Second, feminist social work values emphasize the fundamental equality of women and men and stress women's rights to full economic, political and social opportunities.

Many people still believe that religion prescribes proper behaviours for women that do not include full equality and independence. Social work education and practice generally avoid the issue of religion in women's lives. The need to develop strategies to bridge the gap between traditional religious values and social work values is obvious. There are two complementary challenges for women in social work: to develop a broader comprehensive understanding of religion and its emphasis on social justice and to create an enlarged definition of feminism that highlights freedom of choice.

References

Ahmed, L. 1992. *Women and Gender in Islam: Historical Roots of a Modern Debate*. New Haven and London: Yale University Press.

Balch, D. L. 1981. *Let Wives Be Submissive: The Domestic Code in 1 Peter*. Atlanta GA: Scholars Press.

Brauner, S. 1989. "Martin Luther on Witchcraft: A True Reformer?" in Brink, J., A. P. Coudert and M. C. Horowitz (eds.), *Politics of Gender in Modern Europe*, pp. 29-42.

Carmody, D. L. 1989. *Women and World Religions*, 2nd edition. Englewood Cliffs, NJ: Prentice Hall.

Clark, E. and Richardson, H. (eds.). 1977. *Women and Religion: A Feminist Sourcebook of Christian Thought*. New York: Harper and Row.

Cooey, P., Eakin, W. and McDaniel, J. 1991. *After Patriarchy: Feminist Transformations of the World Religions*. Maryknoll, NY: Orbis Books.

Daly, M. 1968. *The Church and the Second Sex*. New York: Harper Colophon Books.

Daly, M. 1973. *Beyond God the Father: Toward a Philosophy of Women's Liberation*. Boston: Beacon Press.

Douglas, J. 1974. "Women and Continental Reformation," in Ruether, R. (ed.), *Religion and Sexism: Images of Women in the Jewish and Christian Traditions*. New York: Simon and Schuster, pp. 292-318.

Eisenstein, Z. R. 1979. *Capitalist Patriarchy and the Case for Socialist Feminism*. New York and London: Monthly Review Press.

Falk, N. and Gross, R. M. 1989. *Unspoken Worlds: Women's Religious Lives*. Belmont, CA: Wadsworth Publishing Company.

Humm, M. 1989. *The Dictionary of Feminist Theory*. Hemel Hampstead, England: Harvester Wheatsheaf.

McLaughlin, E. 1973. "Equality of Souls, Inequality of Sexes: Women in Medieval Theology," in Ruether, R. (ed.), *Religion and Sexism: Images of Women in the Jewish and Christian Traditions*. New York: Simon and Schuster, pp. 213-266.

Meeks, W. A. (ed.). 1993. *The Harper Collins Study Bible, NRSV*. San Francisco: Harper Collins.

Mernissi, F. 1991. *The Veil and the Male Elite: A Feminist Interpretation of Women's Rights in Islam*. Trans. Mary Jo Lakeland. Reading, Mass.: Addison-Wesley.

Mitchinson, W. 1987. "Early Women's Organizations and Social Reform: Prelude to the Welfare State," in Moscovitch, A. and Albert, J. (eds.), *The Benevolent State: The Growth of Welfare in Canada*. Toronto: Garamond Press.

Prentice, A., Bourne, P., Brandt, G., Light, B., Mitchinson, W. and Black, N. 1988. *Canadian Women: A History*. Toronto: Harcourt, Brace, Jovanovich.

Ruether, R. R. 1974. "Misogyny and Virginal Feminism in the Fathers of the Church," in Ruether, R. (ed.), *Religion and Sexism: Images of Women in the Jewish and Christian Traditions*. New York: Simon and Schuster, pp. 150-183.

Sharma, A. (ed.). 1987. *Women in World Religions*. New York: SUNY Press.

Smith, J. 1987. "Islam," in Sharma, Arvind (ed.), *Women in World Religions*. New York: SUNY Press, pp. 235-250.

Thistlewaite, S. 1985. Every Two Minutes: Battered Women and Feminist Interpretation," in Russell, Letty (ed.), *Feminist Interpretation of the Bible*. Philadelphia: Westminster Press, pp. 96-107.

Trible, P. 1984. *Texts of Terror: Literary-Feminist Readings of Biblical Narratives*. Philadelphia: Fortress.

Wegner, J. 1988. *Chattel or Person? The Status of Women in the Mishnah*. New York: Oxford.

Yee, G. 1989. "I Have Perfumed My Bed With Myrrh: The Foreign Woman (`ssa zara) in Proverbs 1-9." *Journal for the Study of the Old Testament*. 43: 53-68.

Chapter IV
Power and Authority in Social Work

Patricia Taylor

Power and authority are integral parts of the social, legal and ethical context of the social work profession today. Often working fairly independently within the hierarchical structures of social agencies, social workers continue to assume more authority for their practice than they have traditionally. The extent to which social workers understand the nature and power of authority in their profession, and their relationship to it, bears significantly on their effectiveness as professionals. To better understand some problems social workers grapple with in the exercise of authority, the influence of gender needs to be considered.

Social work is a predominantly female profession. As professionals, women have brought, and still bring, into the professional arena the way they have been socialized as females. Gendered socialization affects authority relationships that are generally characterized in terms of dominance and submission. Assertiveness, power and dominance are traits that have been traditionally associated with masculinity, just as nurturing, dependence and submission have been associated with femininity (Broverman et al., 1972; Mackie, 1991). Consequently, one can imply that historically entrenched sex role stereotyping has had a detrimental effect upon women in our society and particularly upon women in the profession of social work. This chapter discusses the consequences of sex role stereotyping and how it directly affects women's personal and professional identities and can ultimately inhibit their expression and use of power and authority as professionals.

The current interest in studying the facts and consequences of gender differences in our society is intriguing as well as problematic. In reviewing the research on the topic one outstanding observation surfaces — the conclusions of psychological and sociological research intended to explain human behaviour largely represent male behaviour. As Mackie put it, "research had been conducted primarily by males (and females who had been socialized to accept the masculine ruling ideas) on topics that interested men, using methods congenial to men" (Mackie, 1991, p. 20). This approach tends to blur the critical issues that are specific to women.

Sociopolitical and economic factors such as the women's movement and the necessity of the double income family have significantly changed women's roles. As a result, changed attitudes, opinions and behaviours are emerging. The percentage of women entering the workforce continues to increase, women as heads of single parent families are on the rise and more women feel less inhibited to become involved in social issues, which coincides with society's greater acceptance of women's views and approval of their achievements. Yet, at the same time, power and authority remain a particular problem for women. Analyzing the historical sex role stereotyping of women will help in understanding this dilemma. It is important to recognize that there are biological and physiological differences between men and women. However, it is equally important to note when and where these differences turn to biases and dictate roles and responsibilities. The most compelling explanation for gender differences involves the concept of sex role stereotyping.

The roots of power and authority in social work are related both to the individual social worker's perception of her personal authority and the external influence of society's values expressed in gendered stereotypes. Stereotyping consists of widely held generalizations and expectations about particular groups that prescribe how members of each group should behave and what characteristics and attitudes they should possess. Sex role stereotyping is the result of assuming that certain attitudes, behaviours and dispositions are associated with gender and that individuals should display such traits in order to be considered well-adjusted. Women are typically described as attractive, emotional, dependent, sensitive and talkative, for example, while men are described as aggressive, tough, confident, rational and enterprising (Williams and Best, 1990). In a profession this may result in a perception that men are more competent than women.

It is evident that Western culture is pervasively patriarchal: men are dominant, more powerful, more valued and have more authority (Hyde, 1985). These entrenched social values and attitudes are historically related to mythology, religion and psychology, all of which promote the notion that men are the norm for human behaviour. Freudian analytic theory classically categorized women as deficient males. Femininity for Freud involved "narcissism, penis envy, a weak superego and masochism" (Steffens, 1990, p. 246). Freud coined the well-known phrase "anatomy is destiny" and often interpreted differences between the sexes in terms of "objective laws of nature," regarding females as the inferior sex rather than considering social constructions. Though biological differences clearly exist, they are heightened by socially constructed normative belief systems. Normative systems have been defined as "culturally provided rules which prescribe appropriate ways of behaving" (Steffens, 1990, p. 247). Most men have been socialized to accept gender differences and use them to their benefit.

From a social learning theory perspective (Bandura, 1986) females are differently reinforced than males for behaviour that is seen as being appropriate for their sex. Violations of gender expectations are perceived as "abnormal" and are punishable often in subtle forms of disapproval or rejection. When girls imitate feminine-modeled nurturing activities, such as cooking or sewing, their actions are seen as being appropriate to the female sex and thus become gender typed.

This type of sex stereotyping occurs early in life, even at birth. Most parents dress their boy and girl infants in different colours (traditionally pink for girls and blue for boys) to distinguish the gender of their newborns. The contemporary diaper industry, for example, has capitalized on parents' desires to dress their boys and girls distinctly by creating gender specific diaper designs — available in blue and pink. In a study of two-year-olds, parents were found to use feminine attributions for girls and masculine attributions for boys. They referred to their daughter's physical attractiveness, nurturing play with dolls, gentleness and doing housework. In contrast, sons were described in reference to their physical and athletic abilities (McGuire, 1988). In the same study it was also noted that fathers took a more active role in gender role socialization of their children, especially their sons. Children between the ages of two and five years are even more extreme and inflexible in their perceptions of gender than adults (Stern and Karraker, 1989), yet most parents seem to be unaware of treating their children in stereotypic ways. Only mothers with nontraditional views seemed to encourage their daughters to be independent (Brooks-Gunn, 1986). For most children, their surroundings are identified by gender. Many children model themselves on the characteristics of their caregiver. Girls are encouraged to be nurturing, accede to authority and be preoccupied with their own attractiveness. In contrast, boys are encouraged to be aggressive, autonomous and attain power. Future occupations such as becoming a nurse for girls or a doctor for boys are often reinforced by parental or peer expectations and play. In a patriarchal society, the end result is a devaluation of women that is internalized by both sexes.

Psychoanalytic theory has associated motherhood with the roots of misogyny (Steffan, 1993). From this perspective sons and daughters in traditional families must both confront maternal power. The mother is the early envied object for both sexes, however, sons are encouraged to reject their mothers and their nurturing qualities in developing their autonomy. Daughters, often under nurtured by their mothers, are also discouraged from strongly identifying with their fathers. Freud asserted that girls envied their father's penis (penis envy) and blamed their mothers for their inherent physical "lack," which lead them to feel guilty and want to be punished (the basis of Freud's theory of female masochism) (Freud, [1993]).

It is no surprise that Freud's theories of femininity have been heavily criticized by feminist thinkers. To the totally vulnerable child, the mother is the source of survival. She is both nurturant and powerful, and the child reacts to deprivation of the mother with fear and anger. As adults, both sexes want to preserve the good nurturing mother and deny the powerful fear-provoking mother. Inevitably, both sexes experience maternal frustration and both mature into adults motivated to construct normative systems that control women's power both in interpersonal relationships and positions of authority in society. From this psychoanalytic perspective, support for a social system powered by men is created.

If we refer back to the concept of the "good mother" being an ideal acknowledged by both sexes, one can understand the negative response that not only men may feel toward the assertive female who strives to assume power and authority but also women who either feel uncomfortable with, or resent and undermine, any woman in power. It also offers some explanation for the feelings of ambivalence experienced by women who achieve roles of power and authority. Even in the domestic sphere, where women are socialized to assume responsibility for family relations, their use of authority in terms of establishing connectedness, nurturing and emotionality are easily negatively stereotyped as being "controlling" or "over involved" or "hysterical" (Walters et al., 1988, p. 28). Two critical features of the female role that stand in direct opposition to power and authority are depression and learned helplessness.

Depression has been linked with powerlessness and lack of control over the direction of one's life. According to Morowsky (1985) women suffer from depression twice as frequently as men. And the women most likely to suffer from mental illness are married with children. Further, it has been strongly suggested that marriage is bad for women's health (Conway, 1990; Morowsky, 1985). Lack of control combined with increasing responsibilities in marriage and on the job increase stress and consequently mental illness, especially depression (Reifman, Beirnat and Lang, 1991). One report even suggests that the stress of combining housework and paid work may be the number one health hazard for women (*Globe and Mail*, 1989). In response, women are prescribed twice as many tranquillizers as men, which hardly serves to alleviate their burden except perhaps to numb women's feelings about it. It is essential to note the double standard that exists in differential evaluation and treatment of women among mental health professionals. Male traits such as competence and assertiveness are thought to represent good mental health and female traits such as dependence and passivity are considered psychopathological. It is not surprising that despite this, behaviour is judged to be adaptive and effective whenever it is consistent with sex typing and maladaptive whenever the situation requires an opposite typed response. Consequently, women are generally accepted in roles that call for affection and caregiving, i.e., female stereotyped behaviours, but not in roles that call for power, authority and assertiveness, because these are typically male sex typed roles (Broverman et al., 1972). Often illnesses diagnosed as pathological can be traced to environmental causes. When we understand the sex role stereotyped expectations of female behaviour coupled with the fact that male behaviour is normative, it is no wonder that women placed in a situation with few behavioural options are prone to depression.

The second feature of sex role stereotyping that is directly connected with depression is learned helplessness. Seligman first identified the theory of learned helplessness in 1967 through a series of investigations into the behaviour of dogs exposed to inescapable shock. He concluded that animals exposed to inescapable shock eventually learned that no behaviour would eliminate the shock. Seligman theorized that in situations where reinforcement is not fixed to behaviour, the animal learns that its behaviour is ineffective. This knowledge results in decreased motivation in later situations where the opportunity to control reinforcement occurs. According to Seligman (1980), this idea has been expanded to explain psychopathology, particularly depression, in humans. Learned helplessness is built into the female stereotype, which is directly connected with high rates of depression in women.

The theory of learned helplessness is not without controversy. Learned helplessness stems from the perceived reality that women still have less control and access to direct power in society than men. It has been shown that women do not reap rewards from the workplace as do men. They are more closely supervised and less likely to be promoted on ability or intelligence than on their efforts to exert influence over their supervisor (Miller, 1992). Though female managers' capacity to reason and make principled judgments is as developed (more so in social work) as men's (Dorbin, 1989), the stereotypic belief that women are incompetent as leaders continues to prevail. One must ask why women are not fairly represented in top management positions. Though many women have risen to middle-management positions, some researchers suggest women are not as comfortable as men in leadership positions simply because they have not had experience with authority (Offerman, 1992). Men are more likely as students to take leadership roles as school editors and in elected or team sports positions. Yet when surveyed, both female and male social work students expressed equal interest in advancing their careers. Interestingly, in one study 59 per cent of the female students and only 4 per cent of the male students believed they would experience discrimination in their job advancement due to gender (Taylor, 1994).

Power has been defined as a struggle to dominate, to have "power over" others. Resistance, conflict, force, domination and control are recurrent themes in patriarchal constructions of the meaning of power (Miller and Cummins, 1992). Yet the traditional concept of power is actually a gender biased one. A majority of women in one study acknowledged that society's definition of power, in terms of money and control over people, was also reflective of a male definition of power (Miller and Cummins, 1992). The concept of empowerment, where participants enhance others' feelings of competence and power, has been endorsed by feminist scholars. However, most women preferred to interpret power for themselves in terms of personal authority or "the power to be self-determining, to act rather than react, to choose the terms on which to live one's own life" (Miller and Cummins, 1992, p. 417) and felt least powerful in a position of dependency. As demonstrated in this study, women largely prefer to experience power in terms of personal authority, expressed as self-control and freedom to make their own choices, rather than to dominate or control others. Women are more innately democratic, preferring caring, responsibility and influence to overt control as some studies have shown (Offerman and Beil, 1992). Some would go so far as to suggest that what constitutes authority for women is exactly what is feared most by men: sustained connectedness (Jones, 1993, p. 158). Women have been long denied access to structural power and are often limited to experiencing traditional power indirectly. Unfortunately, women may find it difficult to exercise personal authority and autonomy without also acquiring the kind of power society sanctions. Perhaps women's power preference of personal authority as opposed to control over others explains in part the cautious view of the management function in social work.

Another interesting theory that influences the gender issue is androgyny. Androgyny suggests "that it is possible for people to exhibit both masculine and feminine qualities" (Sargent, 1985, p. 147). Feminist scholars such as Sandra Bem (1974) proposed that androgyny should replace sex typing as the goal of gender socialization. However, some researchers (Ezell, 1993; Taylor and Hall, 1982) suggest that androgyny contains a bias in that the androgynous female becomes more accepted as she acquires more "masculine" traits. Ezell concludes that women selected for management positions have displayed styles and behaviours that power brokers — who are mostly men — consider important. Women managers may be reacting to expectations to be more "male like" if they wish to be considered good administrators. Consequently, the myth of masculine superiority is maintained and the myth of female inferiority is perpetuated. Certainly, males who acquire more female traits are not considered more socially desirable. Indeed, men are looked down upon if they appear like "women" in physique or character. Given that masculine traits are more socially desirable, it is no wonder that men are prone to feeling insecure about their gender to the point of being homophobic. Unfortunately, it follows that feminine traits are socially inferior to male traits and are undesirable, or even despised, when displayed in women or men. The often overlooked and underlying fact, however, is that men and women have more in common than they are different.

Although many may feel that the growth of the feminist movement and the consciousness raising that gathered momentum in the 1970s have created significant changes for women, it is important to note that feminist writers continue to tell us that we still operate under a patriarchal social structure. Indeed, while women have made strides in the workplace as well as the home, there is evidence that some may have done so at their own cost, frequently taking on the demands of the marketplace in addition to meeting the demands of the home and family. Women often have a double set of responsibilities and few areas of authority. Some women try to cope with their double burden by becoming "superwomen," maintaining traditional domestic responsibilities as well as working outside of the home. Trying to handle both fronts may compromise women's struggle for autonomy and power by clinging to traditionally sanctioned role expectations of "mom" in addition to "breadwinner" besides. However, women's choices are limited. If women don't maintain the home and children, research suggests the job is not likely to get done.

The literature repeatedly reveals that men do much less housework and child care than women (Conway, 1990; Luxton, 1990; Mills et al., 1992). And working women can still expect their employers not only to pay them less and promote them less, but also to consider their family obligations indicative of their lack of commitment to the job. It is no wonder that the most successful women in terms of career are highly educated, between the ages of 35 and 45, single and have no children. The media continues to portray women as having the major responsibility for children with no control, authority or alternative choices, and only the consistent support of products, like quick microwaveable foods and reliable appliances, to help them through. The double burden women experience in juggling their work and domestic responsibilities may strongly influence their decision not to compete for top-level positions. Especially since wives are likely to earn less than their husbands. More women than men continue to abandon their full-time careers for part-time supportive jobs in order to maintain young family needs (Hochschild and Machung, 1989).

Statistics show that much of the workplace is still dictated by the men in authority who outnumber women in power positions by a large margin. Research indicates that females are consistently exposed to roles of lower status and fewer expectations than males. In 1990, Statistics Canada reported that women filled 76 per cent of all clerical, 74 per cent of health (mostly nursing) and 57 per cent of teaching positions. Women only filled 20 per cent of the 10 highest paying jobs in Canada, and their average salary in these positions was only $48,609 compared to $79,463 for men in 1990. Women continue to suffer from pay inequities and a lack of role models. In order to survive in a male dominated marketplace, some women have developed an ability to demonstrate externally compliant behaviour. For example, men and women have different attitudes towards competition. Women, for the most part, are more likely to attain satisfaction from the intrinsic pleasure of task accomplishment, whereas men are more likely to emphasize social comparison and power mastery. Yet women may compete to secure a desired leadership position, although they do not derive the same level of satisfaction from the competition itself as do men (Offerman and Beil, 1992). However, one must question the validity of Offerman and Beil's findings in terms of the total population of women. Some women gain great satisfaction from leadership.

Sex role stereotyping explains why women in our society continue to suffer from low self-esteem, depression and a lack of assertiveness. As a consequence of this stereotyping, there are both personal and social restrictions on women achieving power and exercising authority. Indeed, if one applies the concept of sex role stereotyping to the profession of social work, one can develop a logical reason why the profession continues to grapple with power and authority both within the professional hierarchy and professional practice. Let us look at two professional areas to identify these issues: practice and administration.

The use of authority by social workers is a topic that has concerned the profession for years. Social workers have struggled for a long time with the problem of consolidating their caution about abusing authority with the client's right to self-determination and the dictate to "help the clients help themselves." Social workers are often encouraged to use influence rather than direct power when interacting with their clients (Johnson, 1992, pp. 71-77). Louise Johnson has described it as follows: "A conflict arises when social workers are charged with reconciling their use of authority with client self-determination. Consequently they are cautious about abusing authority and encouraged to use influence rather than power in the therapeutic relationship" (Johnson, 1992, p. 77). Many of them have been frustrated by a profession that stresses client autonomy at the same time it assigns responsibility to the social worker to mandate the client's problems. As Compton and Galaway (1989, p. 296) note, it is no surprise that many social workers have difficulty with the concepts of power and authority and fail to engage their clients. Authority still has negative connotations for numerous social workers because it is perceived to be counterproductive to the helping relationship. However, "nothing so convinces a family that we are dishonest and untrustworthy as our denial of our power and authority" (Compton and Galway, 1989, p. 297). One can identify areas where authority and power are essential to service, such as child protection and the courts. However, the legality that defines these services has frequently been viewed as an obstacle to intervention.

In any discussion on power and authority, empowerment of the client is a critical item. However, empowerment is also problematic. It can suggest to some that while clients acquire the ability to make choices and assume control in their lives, the social worker is disempowered. When social workers, "pretend that they carry no authority [it] leaves clients troubled by suspicion and doubts about why workers are unwilling to admit what they, the clients are so aware of" (Compton and Galaway, 1989, p. 296). As a result, social workers' reluctance to use authority can compromise their ability to engage clients in seeking optimum solutions to their problems. Disparities between professional and organizational goals exist in the social work profession. One could argue that the theories upon which most treatment is based stress a democratic approach to helping. At the same time the norms and standards that dictate practice are often different from those that dictate policy in most bureaucratic agencies.

In legally mandated agencies such as children's aid societies, where society has sanctioned social workers to intervene in the area of parental rights, there is frequently conflict within the agency about use of authority. In bureaucratic settings many social workers "are confronted with the conflict between professional and bureaucratic expectations — with human need, human pain and societal injustices and with agency policy, rules and regulations.... with the slowness of change, the seeming unresponsiveness of the system and demands for accountability by the bureaucratic agency" (Johnson, 1992, p. 210). Many social workers caught in such conflicts suffer considerable stress as their responsibility to intervene professionally is continually superseded by the power and control of the agency. While Johnson suggests that the bureaucratic context of professional practice diminishes the power and authority of the social worker, many women are unaware of the importance of this fact. They are attracted to the profession because of the nurturing, caring approach that social work promotes. This approach is not only naive but may prove to be detrimental to the best interests of the client who cannot avoid the power and authority inherent in the structure of society. Indeed, even the mandate of social work emphasizes action in confronting power and authority in order to assist the client. For example, when a local medical social worker overcame her reluctance to assume authority she confronted the head of the hospital and advocated for the client's need for self-determination over the hospital's need to solve a difficult discharge problem. The social worker reported that as a result of her actions not only was the client pleased but she [the social worker] felt satisfaction in her work and an increased sense of her own competency. Indeed, this is consistent with recent research that has identified a positive relationship between control and mental health (Reifman, Beirnat and Lang, 1991; Morowsky, 1985).

Certainly, it can be concluded that social workers frequently experience conflicts in exercising authority, particularly as they try to reconcile the values and expectations of practice with the demands of society. Social workers do not function without socially approved power and authority, and they must learn to respond to the practice contradictions that exist in the political context. However, there is no political neutrality in social work. Although some social workers may state political neutrality, this statement reflects a political choice. The challenge to social work is to advocate a more just balance of power between the "haves" and the "have nots." However, this task presents many problems to the profession. Some of the most significant ones stem from the fact that social work is predominantly a female profession, and factors associated with power and authority such as assertiveness and dominance are traits associated with males. Traditionally, the nature of authority in social work has been defined by men, and the role of women in relation to authority has been defined as one that incorporates dependence, submission and nurturance (Nemeroff, 1987). Consequently, it follows that the problems with power and authority tend to have been incorporated into the female professional social worker's self. Though some power sharing does exist among professionals in social work, the dominant bureaucratic nature of social welfare organizations tends to diminish the opportunity for egalitarianism and support the passive role of women (Ferguson, 1984, p. 83).

Schools of social work in Canadian universities are reflective of a gendered power imbalance in the profession. Administratively, the most compelling example of inequitable power distributions is identified by examining the faculty, staff and student body. While the profession is made up of approximately three times as many females as males, in general terms, three times as many males as females hold administrative, managerial and/or academic appointments in social work. Indeed, in schools of social work this breakdown is further defined by the differences in rank, with the most obvious one existing at the full professor rank. In 1993, a Canadian Association of Schools of Social Work (CASSW) survey of full-time faculty in 14 Canadian schools of social work, revealed that 17 per cent of full professors were female compared to 33 per cent who were males. The discrepancies within the leadership role of director and/or dean have changed slightly in the last few years. However, there is still an imbalance in favour of males. Females tend to have the largest numbers of students in the largest classes. In the lower professorial ranks, 53 per cent of the positions were occupied by females compared to 27 per cent occupied by males. Certainly, the traditional thinking of needing "the stereotypical strong, assertive male" to lead seems to exist in social work education. The offshoot of this stereotyping also can be seen in the student population. More male students at the MSW level are enrolled in the administration specialization than females. The lack of female role models offers little positive reinforcement to female students who form more than two-thirds of the student body (CASSW, 1993) in schools of social work.

Conclusion

The bottom line suggests that the many factors that define power and authority in our society have had an impact on the status and role women in the profession of social work. Perusal of the literature has shown that sex role stereotyping has defined lower status and expectations in society for females, which, in turn, has a direct impact on issues of power and authority. Within professional practice, social workers experience conflicts that serve to inhibit their professional use of authority and power. Yet, at the same time, power and authority are ideally seen as operating in a cooperative context in the relationship between the worker and the client. One wonders if this interpretation of power and authority has not evolved because the profession is predominantly female. Similarly, one questions the impact of gender on many social work values.

Where power and authority are concerned, the females in the profession suffer from sex role stereotyping. They form the largest segment of the profession yet they are over represented in the lower status jobs and under represented in higher status jobs. If the social worker's professional power and authority is critically related to the social status of the clients (who are predominantly female) it is no wonder that in Ontario, for example, social workers have experienced such a long and unsuccessful battle for legal status. Indeed, one could speculate that the struggle with power and authority that women in social work experience may tend to disempower the female clients they serve. However, things are changing for female social workers. In a society where male competition has traditionally defined corporate success, the collective female action approach is making inroads. Certainly the power of women, as a group, is being felt in the articulation of gender discrimination, in action on job equity, in the identification and prosecution of sexual harassers and the promotion of women's health care. Although the "sisterhood" approach has not replaced the "old boy" network, it does establish a primary power base for women.

In social work education the promotion not only of collegiality between female faculty members but also between female faculty members and female students is creating a new feeling of collective power. Breaking down the traditional structural hierarchy is one way of addressing the power differential. Female students can experience the support of their role models at the same time as they develop individual strategies to strengthen their personal and professional identity. Certainly respect for one another as equal members of a profession is a powerful social statement.

But the struggle is far from over. Opportunities for female social workers to break out of their second-class citizen mould must be created. More female leadership within the profession must be demanded. Female social workers should be encouraged to examine their personal relationship to power and authority within the context of their individual experiences with history, religion, law, culture, education and health care. Only then can women in social work resolve their conflicts with power and authority and identify unique ways to promote equality.

References

Bandura, A. 1986. *Social Foundations of Thought and Action: A Social Cognitive Theory.* Englewood Cliffs, NJ: Prentice-Hall.

Bem, S.L. 1974. "The Measurement of Psychological Androgyny." *Journal of Consulting and Clinical Psychology.* 42: 115-162.

Brooks-Gunn, J. 1986. "The Relationship of Maternal Beliefs about Sex Typing to Maternal and Young Childrens' Behaviour." *Sex Roles.* 15: 2125.

Broverman, I., Broverman, D., Clarkson, F., Rosenkrantz, P. and Vogel, S. 1972. "Sex Role Stereotypes: A Current Appraisal." *Journal of Social Issues.* 28: 3, 59-78.

CASSW. 1993. Unpublished Statistics.

Compton, B. and Galaway, B. 1989. *Social Work Processes,* 4th edition. Belmont, CA: Wadsworth Publishing.

Conway, J. 1990. *The Canadian Family in Crisis.* Toronto: James Lorimar.

Dorbin, A. 1989. "Ethical Judgements of Male and Female Social Workers." *Social Work.* 34: 5, 451-455.

Ezell, M. 1993. "Gender Similarities of Social Work Managers." *Administration in Social Work.* 17: 3, 39-57.

Ferguson, K. 1984. *The Feminist Case Against Bureaucracy.* Philadelphia: Temple University Press, p. 83.

Freud, S. "Femininity." Reprinted in Jagger A. and Rothenburg, P. (1993). *Feminist Frameworks,* Third Edition. New York: McGraw Hill.

Globe and Mail. March 8, 1989. "Stress of Juggling Housework, Job, Called Hazard to Women's Health."

Hochschild, A. and Machung, A. 1989. *The Second Shift: Inside the Two-Job Marriage.* New York: Penguin.

Horner, M. 1970. "Femininity and Successful Achievement: A Basic Inconsistency," in Bardwick, J., E. M. Douvan, M. S. Horner and D. Guttman (eds.), *Feminine Personality and Conflict.* Belmont, CA: Brooks-Cole, pp. 167-188.

Horner, M. 1972. "Toward An Understanding of Achievement Related to Conflicts in Women." *Journal of Social Issues.* 28: 2, 155-175.

Hyde, J. 1985. *Half the Human Experience: The Psychology of Women,* 3rd edition. Lexington: D.C. Heath.

Johnson, L. 1992. *Social Work Practice: A Generalist Approach,* 4th edition. Boston: Allyn and Bacon.

Jones, K.B. 1993. *Compassionate Authority: Democracy and the Representation of Women.* New York: Routledge.

Luxton, M. (ed.). 1990. *Through the Kitchen Window: The Politics of Home and Family.* Toronto: Garamond Press.

Mackie, M. 1991. *Gender Relations in Canada: Further Explorations.* Toronto: Butterworths.

McGuire, J. 1988. "Gender Stereotypes of Parents with Two-Year-Olds and Beliefs about Gender Differences in Behaviour." *Sex Roles.* 19: 233-240.

Miller, C. and Cummins, A. 1992. "An Examination of Women's Perspectives on Power." *Psychology of Women Quarterly.* 16: 4, 415-428.

Miller, J. 1992. "Gender and Supervision: The Legitimation of Authority in Relationship to Task." *Sociological Perspectives.* 35: 1, 137-162.

Mills, R. J., Grasmick, H. G., Morgan, C. S. and Wenk, D. 1992. "The Effects of Gender, Family Satisfaction, and Economic Strain on Psychological Well-Being." *Family Relations.* (October) 41: 440-444.

Morowsky, J. 1985. "Depression and Marital Power: An Equity Model." *American Journal of Sociology.* 91: 557-592.

Nemeroff, G. H. (ed.). 1987. *Women and Men Interdisciplinary Readings on Gender.* Toronto: Fitzhenry and Whiteside, p. 531.

Offerman, L. and Beil, C. 1992. "Achievement Styles of Women Leaders and their Peers." *Psychology of Women Quarterly.* 16: 1, 37-56.

Reifman, A., Beirnat, M. and Lang, E. 1991. "Stress, Social Support, and Health in Married Professional Women with Small Children." *Psychology of Women Quarterly.* 15: 3, 431-445.

Sargent, A. 1985. *Beyond Sex Roles.* St. Paul: West Publishing.

Seligman, M. and Garber, J. (eds.). 1980. *Human Helplessness: Theory and Applications.* New York: Academic Press.

Stern, M. and Karraker, K.H. 1989. "Sex Stereotyping of Infants: A Review of Gender Labelling Studies." *Sex Roles.* 20: 501-522.

Steffens, C. 1993. "Psychoanalysis and Feminism," in Finn, G. (ed.), *Limited Edition: Voices of Women, Voices of Feminism.* Halifax: Fernwood.

Taylor, C. 1994. "Is Gender Inequality in Social Work Management Relevant to Social Work Students?" *British Journal of Social Work.* 24: 2, 157-172.

Taylor, M.C. and Hall, J.A. 1982. "Psychological Androgyny: Theories, Methods and conclusions." *Psychological Bulletin.* 92: 347-366.

Walters, M., Carter, B., Papp, P. and Silverstein, O. 1988. *The Invisible Web: Gender Patterns in Family Relationships.* New York: Guilford Press.

Williams, J. E. and Best, D. L. 1990. *Measuring Sex Stereotypes: A Multination Study.* Newberry Park: Sage.

Chapter V
The Legal Status of Women in Society

Emily F. Carasco

When women and the law courses were first introduced in law schools (in the 1970s), many asked, "Why? Isn't the law the same for men and women?" The response then, as now, is that there are many different ways in which the law has a gender dimension, ways in which it specifically shapes the lives of women. During the last three decades, feminist legal scholars have debunked the myth of the "neutrality" and "objectivity" of the law and have written extensively on feminist legal theory as well as explored substantive areas of law such as criminal law and family law for their treatment of and impact upon women. These writers do not claim that all women experience the law and the legal system in exactly the same manner. Obviously, factors such as race/ethnicity, class and sexual orientation make for a different impact of the law on different groups of women.

The fact is, that the law has not always been the same for men and women. For instance, up until 1925, a husband in Ontario could obtain a divorce on the grounds of his wife's adultery whereas a wife could not obtain a divorce unless she proved that her husband had been guilty of incestuous adultery, rape, sodomy, bestiality, bigamy, adultery coupled with cruelty or adultery coupled with desertion for at least two years. Even where laws are technically the same for women and men, the impact they have on women may be different from the impact they have on men. For example, a legislative requirement that all candidates for police training be six feet tall and weigh 175 lbs. clearly excludes large numbers of woman (and some minority groups). Apart from the impact of gender on substantive areas of the law, the very nature of the law, the processes in the legal system and the interpretation of the law has been affected by the dominant role played by men and the relatively minor role played by women in the political and legal system. In 1990, Madame Justice Bertha Wilson, then a Supreme Court Justice, sent shock waves through the legal profession by openly stating what feminist lawyers had known for a long time: "[That] many studies have found overwhelming evidence that gender-based myths, biases and stereotypes are deeply imbedded in the attitudes of many male judges, as well as in the law itself."

The purpose of this chapter is to focus on some of the important ways in which the lives of women in Canada have been directed and deeply affected by the beliefs, prejudices, likes and dislikes, ideals and plans of mostly male law-makers (legislators) and mostly male interpreters of the law (judges). There is little in both the public spheres and private spheres of women's lives that is not touched by the law. Any attempt by women and men of goodwill to fully emancipate women or even to merely understand the legal status of women in our society, must be accompanied by some knowledge both of the history of the law as a tool of oppression and of its potential and use as a tool of liberation. This chapter is a modest attempt to provide a beginning on the subject. In parts of this chapter where substantive law has been discussed, it is by no means a comprehensive coverage of the subject area. The subjects were selected because they are illustrative of the influence of the law on the lives of women and because they involve situations that may involve the intervention of social work.

Formal Equality Under the Law: Women as Persons

Since 1982, Canadian women have been guaranteed equality before and under the law through Sec. 15 of the Canadian Charter of Rights and Freedoms. Formal equality under the law should not be taken for granted. It is important to be aware that women have not always had equality in the law. For example, unlike Canadian men, women could not become lawyers until 1897 (in Ontario); could not vote in federal elections until 1918; could not hold political office and sit in Parliament until 1920. A turning point for Canadian women was the debate in the 1920s as to whether women could be considered "legal persons," or be included within definitions of "person" or "man" in legislation governing various professional and civic rights and duties. In the now famous Persons Case (Edwards v. Attorney General for Canada 1928; 1930) five prominent Canadian women brought a reference to the Supreme Court of Canada for interpretation of the sections in the British North America Act, 1867, which covered eligibility to be called as Senators. The section referred to "qualified persons" as being eligible and thus, the issue was whether woman were "persons" recognized in law. The Supreme Court of Canada ruled that women are not among the "qualified persons" who may be called to the Senate under the terms of the British North America Act, since that Act was passed in 1867 when woman had no legal capacity. The matter was taken on appeal to the Privy Council in England, at that time the highest court of appeal for legal disputes in the Commonwealth. The Privy Council held that women were indeed legal persons in 1930, even if not so defined at earlier times.

Obtaining legal personhood did not guarantee female persons the same treatment under the law as that accorded to male persons. Discrimination against women continued to be rampant in many spheres but probably none so glaringly as in the workplace. Employers could still deny employment to women on the basis of sex, and they did not have to pay men and women equally in the same workplace. In 1953, the Canada Fair Employment Practices Act prohibited discrimination based on sex in the hiring of employees, and in 1956, the Female Employers Equal Pay provided for equal pay for women doing "identical or substantially identical work" to men for the same employer. Women still earn only 70 cents for every dollar men earn, and women generally are still located within the low-paying wage sectors and are at junior levels even in better paying sectors. Pay equity legislation has helped somewhat, but many feminists believe that until there is mandatory employment equity legislation with firm numerical goals, employers will continue to discriminate against women.

It was not until 1960 that the Canadian Bill of Rights prohibited any kind of discrimination based on sex. Legal prohibition of discrimination could not, and did not, eliminate discrimination. In 1967, recognizing that women still experienced discrimination on various levels, the federal government appointed the Royal Commission on the Status of Women in Canada to investigate and recommend steps "to ensure for women equal opportunities with men in all aspects of Canadian society."

The Canadian Bill of Rights proved to be an imperfect tool for women's equality claims. For instance, it was of no help to native women who challenged the discriminatory sections of the Indian Act as being contrary to the provisions of the Bill. Under the Indian Act, Indian women who married non-Indians lost their band status, but Indian men did not lose their status if they married non-Indian women. It was held that the Bill of Rights could not override the Indian Act. It was not until equality provisions were entrenched in the Canadian Constitution's Charter of Rights and Freedoms that this discrimination against native women was eliminated.

The entrenchment of the Canadian Charter of Rights and Freedoms in the 1982 Constitution, especially section 15, heralded a new attempt by government to ensure equality for women. This section served the purpose of imposing formal equality for women under the law. It has also been used to challenge a number of discriminatory laws and has led to some ground-breaking cases on equality and discrimination. Formal equality is only the first step and even a cursory examination of a few areas of substantive law reveal how much remains to be changed.

Family Law

Spousal support

A number of authors have commented on the ways in which family law has historically reinforced societal assumptions about the status and roles of women. An area that clearly demonstrates this fact is the law governing the property rights of spouses upon the breakdown of a marriage. Since the mid 80s, Canadian provinces began to provide for an equal sharing, upon breakdown of a marriage, of all property acquired during the marriage. In Ontario for instance, the Family Law Act 1986 provides that spouses are entitled to an equal share of the total financial product of the marriage, which is determined by calculating the net family property of each spouse when the marriage relationship ends. In order to fully grasp the significance of the current law governing the property rights of spouses upon marriage breakdown, some knowledge of the historical background of this law is necessary.

A series of married women's property acts were introduced in the nineteenth century to make it possible for wives to acquire and hold property. Prior to that the common law doctrine of legal personality decreed that upon marriage the husband and wife became one legal personality. In effect, that personality was the husband. He acquired the right to manage and control all of the wife's freehold land (if she had any) and he was entitled to the rent and profits. A wife was unable to dispose of her land without his consent and she had no right to contract, to sue or be sued. The married women's property acts eliminated property rights created by marriage. In matters relating to ownership of property a husband and wife were to be treated as strangers, that is, if either owned property in his or her name, that person was entitled to keep it or dispose of it as he or she chose. Upon breakdown of a marriage, the owner of the property retained that property and was under no obligation to share it with his or her spouse. The system of separate property for the most part resulted in severe hardship for the wife when a marriage ended. The traditional role of breadwinner and money manager for the family was assumed by the husband: since the vast majority of women at the time were not employed outside the home, this usually meant that any property accumulated during a marriage was paid for by the husband and registered in his name. Therefore according to the scheme of separate property, it belonged to him absolutely. While a marriage continued, this did not create any problems generally. When the marriage broke down, the wife frequently had no property and no rights to any of her husband's property.

Apart from a few isolated instances of judicial intervention, this inequitable system of separate property continued for over 100 years. It took a case of shocking injustice to bring about legal reform. In 1975, the Supreme Court of Canada heard a case involving a couple who had been married for 25 years. Shortly after their marriage in 1943, the Murdochs worked on ranches as a hired couple. Later they operated a guest ranch. In 1951 with the proceeds of the sale of the guest ranch, and a loan from Mrs. Murdoch's mother, Mr. Murdoch acquired a valuable ranch in his name alone. From that time until their separation in 1968, Mrs. Murdoch continued to work on the ranch and her husband continued to maintain outside employment. At trial, Mrs. Murdoch testified that she was involved in "haying, raking, swathing, mowing, driving trucks and tractors and teams, quietening horses, taking cattle back and forth to the reserve, dehorning, vaccinating, branding, anything that was to be done." After separation in 1968, Mrs. Murdoch claimed an interest in the ranch. The majority of the Supreme Court upheld the trial judge's holding that Mrs. Murdoch's contribution could be characterized as the performance of the usual duties of matrimony and did not give rise to a legal claim on the property in her husband's name. After 25 years of hard work as both a rancher and homemaker, Mrs. Murdoch was left poor, her husband wealthy.

The failure, inability or unwillingness of the judiciary to remedy the harsh consequences of the separate property regime led to provincial legislative reform. In Ontario, the 1978 Family Law Reform Act provided for the general retention of separate property during marriage, but upon separation family assets, including the matrimonial home, were to be divided. In certain specified circumstances, nonfamily assets could also be divided. The Family Law Reform Act was a considerable improvement on the separate property regime but it was seriously flawed. Though entitlement was based on the concept of marriage as a partnership in which each spouse contributes in various ways to the financial gain of both spouses, only assets used for family purposes were subject to division. Once again women were placed at a disadvantage particularly in situations where they were homemakers and their husbands worked outside the home. These women were limited to assets used for family purposes during the marriage. If family savings went into property or assets not used for family purposes, for example, a family business in the husband's name, this property was not automatically included in the division of assets. Furthermore, important assets such as pensions and retirement savings plans in the name of the earning spouse were held not to be family assets. The results of this approach were particularly hard on women from low-income households who separated after a long marriage. They frequently got little or nothing in the way of a share of family assets.

The 1986 Ontario Family Law Act, the current law, was premised on the assumption that both spouses make a vital and essentially equal contribution to the economic viability of the family unit and to the acquisition of wealth by the family unit. Therefore, a spouse is entitled to an equal share of the total financial product of the marriage. For financially independent women and/or women who are in marriages where the total assets of the unit are considerable, this approach is of course far more equitable than the limited family assets division under the now defunct 1978 Family Law Reform Act. Unfortunately, significant numbers of married women either do not have an independent income and/or will not get enough in the division of net family property to maintain themselves and their dependants upon breakdown of the family unit. To understand the failure of the legal system to adequately respond to the financial plight of these women, one must examine the law of spousal support.

In the late 60s and 70s major changes took place in the federal and provincial law governing spousal support. Prior to this period a woman could obtain spousal support if she could prove that her husband was guilty of a matrimonial offence (for example, desertion, adultery) and if she herself was blameless. A wife's faulty behaviour could mean partial or total denial of financial support. Husbands had no right to claim support. With the 1968 Divorce Act, Canada got its first national divorce law and it changed the face of spousal support forever. Either husband or wife could claim support and the claimant no longer had to allege fault or be faultless. Provincial laws were influenced by the changes expressed in the Divorce Act and went a step further. In Ontario for instance, the Family Law Reform Act held each spouse to have an obligation to support himself or herself, to be self-supporting, and if support was claimed upon a marriage breakdown, it had to be based on financial need and not on an assumption that a marriage certificate guaranteed maintenance. The 1985 federal Divorce Act, currently the divorce law, picked up on the provincial trend and enshrined the principle of self-sufficiency.

Within 20 years, three core elements of spousal support law in Canada (presumed economic dependency of wives, fault and the right to spousal support) were replaced by three new tenets: self-sufficiency, need and equality. The rationale for this dramatic shift was as follows. First, the role of women in society was changing and there was a desire to eliminate the assumption that a wife was inherently dependent on her husband. Second marriages were becoming increasingly common and finally, the view that every marriage created a right to maintenance for the rest of one's life was abhorrent to many. Hence, the obligation for each person in a marriage to maintain oneself was promoted. Nevertheless there was recognition that upon a marriage breakdown a spouse may have financial need, and a claim for support should be permitted without regard to conduct and that the other spouse had the primary obligation to support the dependant spouse to the best of his or her ability.

The new philosophy of self-sufficiency during a marriage and upon breakdown of a marriage has not resulted in equality in outcome for many women. The courts attempted to encourage self-sufficiency by awarding no spousal support or short-term support awards. The goal of maintenance became rehabilitative, awards being made for such periods as the judge deemed necessary for the dependant spouse to adjust to his or her new economic circumstances. The question of what exactly constitutes "self-sufficiency" or whether this is a feasible goal for all women has never been adequately addressed by the legislation or by judges.

Two groups are particularly hard hit by the contradictions between the goal of self-sufficiency and the reality of the marketplace. The first group are women in their forties and fifties who divorce after a long-term marriage where they played the role of the traditional wife — 20 per cent of all divorces. These women will most likely find low-paying jobs. For example, the following hypothetical case is based on an actual family in Manitoba. The wife had few employable skills after a 27-year marriage and was only able to secure a clerical job paying $13,000 per year. Her husband was earning over $36, 000 per year. The judge gave no maintenance as the couple's assets had already been shared equally under the province's marital property legislation. He assumed this division made the wife financially independent. Both spouses were in their early fifties but the result of this decision is, the husband increased his standard of living substantially; he now keeps all his salary for himself and retains his share of their assets to invest or enjoy. The wife on the other hand, must erode her share of their assets to supplement her low income. She has no ability to plan a secure economic future and her prospects for future career advancement are slight.

The second group of women to be disadvantaged by blind adherence to the goal of self-sufficiency are women in their mid to late thirties who have custody of young children — 40 per cent of all divorces. Given the lack of adequate child care facilities, the quantum of child support awards, which rarely amount to even half of the direct costs associated with children and are poorly enforced, these women are generally unable to cope with the demand to become economically self-sufficient. A new class of poor — divorced women and their children — has been created, and one out of six families with children headed by women are in financial difficulty. Judicial discretion is not limited to the question of self-sufficiency. There is the question of what constitutes "needs" arising from the marriage. For instance, does the word "need" refer to subsistence level need or is it based on the standard of living previously enjoyed? Should a dependant spouse be supported until she completes a vocational re-training program or when she reaches a salary level that would allow her to maintain herself as she might have been able to do had she remained in the workplace?

These questions and others were discussed in a 1983 Supreme Court of Canada decision, Messier v. Delage. Upon obtaining a divorce in 1975, the wife in this case was awarded time-limited support. She embarked on a course of study and acquired a masters degree in translation. While she was able to obtain part-time employment, market conditions made it impossible for her to find full-time employment. In 1979, the husband applied to have spousal support terminated. Three members of the Supreme Court held that the husband's obligations ended when his former wife obtained retraining. The fact that the wife was now employable, albeit unemployed, was a social problem and was not related to the marriage. The majority decision stressed the need to make individual decisions according to the facts of the particular case and was in favour of continued periodic support. They appeared to acknowledge the connection between the wife's continued unemployment and the marriage. Generally speaking however, the breadth of judicial discretion involved in spousal support laws does not appear to have worked in favour of women.

Violence Against Women

One aspect of women in contact with the criminal justice system will be discussed, and that is the subject of wife assault. A 1985 Canada-wide study estimated that almost one million women are assaulted each year. Of all women murdered in Canada, 62 per cent are killed by their partners. Of the 17,300 sexual assault incidents in Canada in 1981, 90 per cent involved female victims and fewer than 4 per cent were reported to the police. Various studies have indicated that lack of confidence in the legal system is one of the reasons for women's reluctance to report attacks. The magnitude of the problem is such that eliminating the shortcomings of the legal system's response to violence against women will not be sufficient. A multi-faceted response including a national violence-prevention education campaign and adequate funding for agencies providing support services for abused women is desperately needed.

Until recently, the response of the criminal justice system to wife assault was poor. For example, until 1955 the Canadian Criminal Code included wife beating as a distinct category of assault under which a man could be punished by imprisonment only if he inflicted actual bodily harm on his wife. An assault charge against anyone else could be laid even if there was only an attempt or a threat of violence. Violence within marriage was regarded for the most part as a private matter and the legal system only intervened in the most serious cases. It is noteworthy that the extensive 1970 Report of the Federal Royal Commission on the Status of Women failed to mention the issue of violence against women.

The women's movement was the main impetus for a change in attitude toward tolerance of abuse against women. A 1980 study on "Wife Battering in Canada" published by the Canadian Advisory Council on the Status of Women stated that every year one in ten Canadian women who are married or in a relationship with a live-in lover are battered. Attention was finally drawn to the fact that the reported cases were only the tip of the iceberg. One study showed that on average women spoke of enduring ten physical assaults before they sought outside help. Clearly the legal system was not responding well to their problem.

Advocates for the elimination of wife battery exposed the fact that the police were often reluctant to press charges against the perpetrators of wife abuse; that the battered woman syndrome was far more complex than was earlier recognized; that battered wives often expressed the view that criminal charges leading to the imprisonment of the breadwinning spouse was not the best option for the family; that crown attorneys and judges frequently did not treat the crime with the seriousness it deserved; that the trial of the alleged perpetrator was often a humiliating, difficult and painful process for the victim…. Despite this women continue to demand a strong and decisive action on the part of the criminal justice system. There is also general acknowledgement that the current system with its punitive and adversarial culture requires radical changes to appropriately respond to the specifically gender- based crime of wife assault.

Meanwhile, some of the key sectors of the criminal justice system have responded to the concerns raised by women. Two major legislative changes have taken place in recent years. As of 1983, the sexual assault legislation was changed: a husband could be charged with raping his wife. Later in 1983, amendments to the Canada Evidence Act made it possible for a spouse to give evidence against her or his spouse in relation to offences such as wife battering and child abuse. Perhaps the most significant change has occurred in the vigour with which police and crown attorneys now approach the issue of charging in wife-battering cases. On July 15, 1982, a letter was sent by the federal Ministry of the Solicitor General to the Executive of the Canadian Association of Chiefs of Police requesting their support and cooperation in dealing with violence in the family, and encouraging all Canadian police forces to lay charges. As well, since 1982 all provincial/ territorial governments have issued directives to the police and in most case to crown attorneys as well, encouraging rigorous investigation and prosecution of wife-battering cases. The positive results are not uniform throughout the country, but the situation for victims has improved. A tremendous amount remains to be done in continued education and training for the police, lawyers and judges on the subject of battered women.

The Supreme Court decision in R. Lavallee in 1990 provides a dramatic example of the influence of women's activism on the law. In that case the Court recognized that a history of violent abuse in a relationship is relevant to measuring reasonableness in self-defence. In that case, Lyn Lavallee had been beaten so brutally that she had had to go to hospital eight times in three years and had suffered injuries that ranged from a split lip, broken nose and black eyes to broken ribs and multiple cuts and bruises. Madame Justice Bertha Wilson specifically recognized the battered woman syndrome, which she believed explained why Lyn Lavallee could not be held responsible for her abuser's violence and why she stayed in the relationship despite the violence. Physical abuse has been around for a long time, but the particular impact of spousal abuse on women has only recently been explored, studied and publicized.

Legislators and Judges

Our laws and our legal system are very much the product of male influences and ideas. In Canada, even today, women make up less than 20 per cent of the House of Commons. Given that women are now 44 per cent of the paid workforce and that in addition women perform $200 billion worth of unpaid work in the home annually, women are not participating in law-making in proportion to their contribution to the country's economy. Western European countries such as Denmark and Sweden are outstanding examples of better laws for women when there is greater participation by women in law-making.

Women don't feature prominently in the judiciary. Currently, over 90 per cent of the federally appointed judges are male persons from a fairly homogenous class background. Every day this small group makes decisions that impact upon every aspect of the lives of millions of people whose life experiences are very different from their own. A more diverse judiciary, more representative of society, could only enrich the bench.

Clearly there is a subjective element in making judicial decisions. Judges are influenced not only by the persuasive legal reasoning and logic but also by their own experiences, likes, dislikes and prejudices. For example, in making family law decisions, particularly in areas that are open to judicial discretion, the individual judge's views about the role of women in our society will undoubtedly impact upon the decision. A prominent judge in Ontario has stated that every decision-maker who walks into a courtroom to hear a case is armed not only with the relevant legal texts but with a set of values, experiences and assumptions that are thoroughly embedded in oneself. If these values are discriminatory to women, the law becomes an instrument of the continued oppression of women; if the values are predominantly those of a small minority, society is being denied the benefit of the best of the values from all segments of the society.

Would more women in the judiciary make a difference? Madame Justice Bertha Wilson, the first woman to be appointed to the Supreme Court of Canada, has answered this question in the affirmative. Women would bring a whole different set of experiences, values and assumptions to judicial decision-making.

Carol Gilligan in her book, *In a Different Voice*, concludes that women think differently from men, particularly in responding to moral dilemmas. According to her, they have different ways of thinking about themselves and their relationships to others. Even if one does not accept this conclusion, it is entirely discriminatory to exclude women's participation in judicial decision-making.

There are other ways in which women on the bench would make a difference. Their presence on the bench would play an important part in eroding the stereotypes about women's role in our society. Judges are among the most highly respected persons in our society and having more women judges would undoubtedly help elevate the status of women. As many would testify, courtrooms can be intimidating, cold places. If the physical image of judges changed such that it would be more representative of our society as a whole, it is likely that the courtroom would become less alienating. Some women lawyers and witnesses have been subjected to humiliating incidents of sexism at the hands of male judges. More female judges would not only decrease the risk of this happening but would also alter the now almost exclusively male culture of the judiciary.

Some provinces, Ontario in particular, have made impressive inroads into diversifying the profile of provincially appointed judges. Meanwhile, sexist comments made by a number of judges, as well as substantive decisions that indicate little understanding of the context in which women operate, make it imperative that judges undertake gender bias education. Our society is changing rapidly. If judges are to make just decisions, they must engage in a career-long study of the social, economic and political phenomena in society.

Conclusion

For a long time leading up to the Charter of Rights and Freedoms women have demanded equality. Section 15 of the Charter guarantees women equality before the law. However, treating men and woman alike when they are differently situated in our society does not necessarily lead to justice. In the attempt to achieve equality between men and women, differences of race, ethnicity, class and sexual orientation among women were often ignored. These factors are part of the context that the law expects and therefore may make for unequal or unjust results. The law must be constantly and carefully scrutinized not only to continually ensure fairness in the legislation but also fairness in the application and the result. Thanks to the work of many feminist lawyers, the legal struggle has moved beyond achieving formal equality in the law to achieving equity for women, by demanding that the law recognize that women are different but not inferior.

References

Abell, J. and Geller, G. (eds.). 1985-86. *Women and the Criminal Justice System, a Special Issue of Resources for Feminist Research*. 14: 4.

Baines, B. 1981. "Women, Human Rights and the Constitution," in Doerr, Audrey and Micheline Carrier (eds.), *Women and the Constitution*. Ottawa: Canadian Advisory Council on the Status of Women, 31.

Boyle, C. 1985. "Sexual Assault and the Feminist Judge." *Canadian Journal of Women and the Law*. 1: 93.

Canada. 1970. *Report of the Royal Commission on the Status of Women in Canada*. Ottawa: Information Canada.

Canada. 1984. *Report of the Royal Commission on Equality in Employment*. Ottawa: Minister of Supply and Services.

Dawson, T. B. 1985. "Legal Structures: A Feminist Critique of Sexual Assault Reform." *Resources for Feminist Research*. 14: 3, 40.

Eberts, M. 1984. "Sex and Equality Rights," in Bayefsky, Anne and Mary Eberts (eds.), *Equality Rights and the Canadian Charter of Rights and Freedoms*. Toronto: Carswells, p. 183.

Gavigan, S. (forthcoming). "Law, Gender and Ideology" in Bayefsky, Anne, (ed.), *Legal Theory Meets Legal Practice*. Edmonton: Academic Printing and Publishing.

Gavigan, S. 1986. "Women, Law and Patriarchal Relations: Perspectives Within the Sociology of Law" in Boyd, Neil (ed.), *The Social Dimensions of Law*. Scarborough: Prentice Hall, p. 101.

Greschner, D. 1985. *The Full Implementation of Equality*. Ottawa: Canadian Advisory Council on the Status of Women.

Hughes, P. (forthcoming). "Feminist Equality and the Charter: A New World View." *Windsor Yearbook of Access to Justice*.

Jain, H. C. 1982. "Race and Sex Discrimination in Employment in Canada." *Relations Industrielles*. 37: 344.

Jamieson, K. 1978. *Indian Women and the Law in Canada: Citizens Minus*. Ottawa: Canadian Advisory Council on the Status of Women.

Lahey, K. 1985. "...until women themselves have told us all there is to tell..." *Osgoode Hall Law Journal*. 23: 519.

Mahoney, K. E. 1985. "Daycare and Equality in Canada." *Manitoba Law Review*. 14: 305.

Mossman, M. J. 1985. "Gender, Equality and the Charter." *Research Studies of the Commission on Equality in Employment*. Ottawa: Minister of Supply and Services, p. 299.

Ng, R. 1980. "The Politics of Ontario's Family Law Reform Act." *Canadian Woman Studies*. 2: 4, 86.

Niemann, L. 1984. *Wage Discrimination and Women Workers: The Move Towards Equal Pay for Work of Equal Value in Canada*. Ottawa: Labour Canada, Women's Bureau.

Pask, E. D. et al. (eds.). 1985. *Women, the Law, and the Economy*. Toronto: Butterworths.

Reaume, D. 1979. "Women and the Law: Equality Claims Before Courts and Tribunals." *Queen's Law Journal*. 5: 3.

Schmid, C. 1978. "The Changing Status of Women in the United States and Canada: An Overview." *Sociological Symposium*. 15: 1.

Sloss, E. (ed.). 1985. *Family Law in Canada: New Directions.* Ottawa: Canadian Advisory Council of the Status of Women.

Vickers, J. M. 1983. "Major Equality Issues of the 80's." *Canadian Human Rights Yearbook.* 1: 47.

Wilson, B. 1983. "Law In Society: The Principle of Sexual Equality." *Manitoba Law Journal.* 13: 221.

Chapter VI
Encountering or
Countering Women Abuse

Joan Pennell

Without a feminist mentor, social workers too often accept without question conventional beliefs on gender roles and the nature of families and are unable to identify the systemic causes and functions of women abuse. The result is that when social workers come upon women abuse, these remain "encounters" or unexpected meetings. Feminist teachings reorient social workers to perceive how sexism twists what should be mutually caring relations into their opposite — abuse. This chapter outlines major feminist teachings on how to "counter" or stop women abuse and proposes three principles to guide social workers in enacting them.

As social workers, we can point to our past and current theories, policies and practices that perpetuate women abuse. Such criticism can mire us in defeatist thinking unless we also identify ourselves as learners shaped by and shaping our involvements. Our "teachers," whether in the home, school, workplace or community, influence how we view and respond to women abuse. Deviating from their dictums can lead to internal uncertainties and externally imposed penalties. Alternative teachers are required who can offer us the frameworks and supports that help us develop and test new approaches. For some Canadian social workers, the women's movement has served in such a capacity. We have not only been recipients of feminist teachings but also full participants, that is simultaneously teachers and students, in the women's movement. In this dual position, we have witnessed how our profession has grown through the contributions of the women's movement and how it has reabsorbed these gains into standard practices that perpetuate women abuse.

Without a feminist mentor, social workers, whether they are based in social systems or "radical" theory, too often accept without question conventional beliefs on gender roles and the nature of families (Marchant, 1986). Adoption of these views ill prepares us either to recognize or to redress women abuse (Maynard, 1985). The result is that when social workers come upon women abuse, as we frequently do in our work, these remain "encounters" or unexpected meetings. As long as women abuse remains an incident, we are not oriented to "counter," that is stop, the violence. We need to recognize that women abuse is not the accidental release of anger but an intentional coercion to intimidate and control one's intimate, female partner through a variety of means, whether physical force, sexual assault, emotional degradation or social isolation; that it is not the momentary mis-expression of romantic love but a fundamental betrayal of trust in a relationship supposedly based upon mutual caring; and that it is not isolated events but instead a recurring pattern in individual lives across Canadian society.

Our teachers do not simply pass on ideas or beliefs; they also exemplify ways of engaging with the world. It is these learned processes that most affect the manner in which we conduct ourselves as social work practitioners. Our teachings provide direction on how to talk, think and act in regards to women abuse. Conventional teachings lead us to encounter this phenomenon, and feminist teachings reorient us to counter it.

This chapter is devoted to looking at the manner in which involvement in the women's movement has helped us as social workers to reconsider our approach to violence against women. Abuse is explained by considering how its opposite, caring, has been constricted and twisted by sexism. The impact of conventional and feminist teachings on social workers' dialogue, analysis, and action regarding women abuse are contrasted. The chapter concludes with an explication of the meaning of feminist teachings for social work efforts to counter women abuse and promote mutual caring.

Conventional and Feminist Teachings

"Conventional teachings" here refer to the imparting of liberal thinking that advocates the advancement of individual rights and equal opportunities while simultaneously embedding women and children within the family. Living this contradiction, women and girls are expected both to take charge of their own destinies and to give of themselves to others. Liberalism enjoins women to adhere to the work ethic of self-sufficiency and the family ethic of caregiving despite the fact that the responsibility for the latter continues to fall almost exclusively on the shoulders of women (Abramovitz, 1988). Today, the rhetoric of "shared parenting" has increased, but women continue to do the vast majority of the housework and child care despite their increased involvement in the paid workforce (Luxton et al., 1990; Sinclair and Felt, 1992). Although the reassertion of fatherhood in the 1980s has justified men taking greater control over domestic life, men who attempt to engage in a practical manner in these activities are discouraged by their relatives, peers and colleagues and inhibited by their socialization from expressing emotions and closeness (Segal, 1990).

Family responsibilities disadvantage women in the labour market as they must adjust their paid work to their domestic obligations; and low or no earnings render women dependent on male breadwinners or state welfare. Moreover, the assumption that caregiving is the natural role of women leads to the discounting of such labour as work whether in the home or workplace (Baines, Evans and Neysmith, 1991). Housewives are uncompensated, and service workers, including social workers, are inequitably remunerated. The numerous changes in Canadian family, labour and welfare policies have served to prop up sexist family norms within a competitive marketplace (Ursel, 1992).

Devaluation of women's caring not only sets women as well as their children and other dependents at risk of poverty but also of abuse (Callahan, 1993). Given their economic insecurities and familial responsibilities, women are positioned neither to care for nor protect themselves and their dependents. Battered women are repeatedly blamed by state agencies for neglecting their charges. The focus on inadequate mothering turns attention away from structural issues such as poverty, racism, heterosexism and ableism and forestalls the creation of a network of relations in which children and their caregivers receive adequate support and protection. Thus, the state's role of protecting all its citizenry is transposed into social controls over the victim of abuse rather than the perpetrator.

The invisibility of women's caregiving in industrialized societies permits men to expect such service without acknowledging their dependency upon it. The masculine persona of strength, self-sufficiency and autonomy remains unchallenged, and men's dominance over their female partners is viewed as a right. Significantly, male violence escalates when men perceive threats to their control. Jealous fears that the woman is having an affair with another man are a commonly cited reason for violence. Women are at particular risk during pregnancy, a time when many men feel displaced by the growing fetus (Hoff, 1990). The danger and lethality of the abuse rises when women threaten to leave or separate from their abuser (Wilson and Daly, 1994) to the extent now that lawyers are being cautioned about "separation assault" (Mahoney, 1991).

"Feminist teachings" offer an alternative perspective on caregiving. They assert that those who are expected to be the caregivers in our society warrant caring. While the young child's needs must often be addressed first, women's requirements, aspirations and commitments are always acknowledged. Building on this awareness, social workers can work with others to develop what Karen Swift refers to as a system of "collective caring" in which "those who provide care and those who receive care are part of a reciprocal network" (Swift, 1991, p. 264). Mothers are not left alone with their children to meet standards of caring. Instead, communal approaches are established in which girls and boys can experience and grow into caring. While change among men progresses in "slow motion," some men have demonstrated their capacity to overcome masculine codes of manhood and engage in egalitarian partnerships (Segal, 1992).

In Canada, various aboriginal communities have taken the lead in regaining their sense of "community-mindedness"; they seek to reclaim their traditions that sustain the involvement of the extended family in caring for all of its members (Hodgson and "Phyllis," 1990, p. 35). Such a cooperative approach makes it possible to move beyond blaming individuals to addressing systemic injustices and affirming one's heritage. And it offers guidance in effecting a system in which the family, community and government can work together to exert social controls that prevent or halt abuse.

The women's movement has learned to advocate simultaneously respecting different cultures and eradicating oppression in any culture. Rather than imposing external standards on how people should relate with each other, the meaning of caring and abuse is sought within their cultural context. It is, however, not assumed that a culture holds a uniform set of norms. The aim is to listen to a full range of voices and to create contexts in which those who have been accorded the least power can formulate and articulate their opinions in safety. To work out their stance, people commonly need the opportunity to gather with others in similar situations and to contrast and invigorate their views with alternative perspectives.

Particular attention needs to be focused on points where people identify contradictions so that they can think through their own positions. An example is given in a study (Pilowsky, 1993) of Spanish-speaking women living in Toronto. These women moved from denial to acknowledgement of their partner's abuse when they confronted two competing moral premises from within their culture: that a good woman sacrifices herself for her family and that no one, including their husbands, should hurt those whom they love. By juxtaposing these two messages, the women arrived at the position that they also warranted respect and caring.

Encountering Versus Countering

For heuristic purposes, social work interventions into women abuse are divided into those that encounter and those which counter. This dichotomy is used as a beginning point from which to explore the relationship between our teachings and practice approaches. Figure 1 depicts how conventional teachings reinforce "encountering" women abuse and feminist teachings redirect social workers to "countering" it.

Figure 1

The Impact of Conventional and Feminist Teachings on Women Abuse Interventions

Conventional Teachings	Encountering Women Abuse	Feminist Teaching	Countering Women Abuse
Keeping Secrets ➡	Individualize and Isolate	Sharing Stories ➡	Identify Affinities
Uncritical Thinking ➡	Minimize and Normalize	Consciousness Raising ➡	Uncover Systemic Oppression
Reaction ➡	Fragment Strategy	Reflective Action ➡	Unify Strategy

The figure attends first to expected patterns of communication because these norms limit what we intervene into and what we can raise as issues for public consideration. The effect on social work practice of "keeping secrets" is compared with that of "sharing stories." As social workers we are expected to respect the privacy of others, the difficulty with our training is that it can lead us to perpetuate what Sandra Butler (1985) refers to as the "conspiracy of silence." Unless we work to create forums for open and safe discussion, people remain isolated, unable to define or "name" their own experiences and become stuck with labels imposed by others. By listening to the experiences of those from diverse walks of life, we come to recognize common causes and move beyond individualizing abuse as the problem of a particular woman or societal group. At the same time, we also avoid homogenizing the experiences of violence. By hearing about differences whether of situation, history or culture we develop a sense of affinity or connection while avoiding an assumption of sameness.

Relaying experiences is the first step toward building a collective effort to stop violence; the second step is analyzing these experiences. We need to move from "uncritical thinking," where we do not question the causes and functions of women abuse, to "consciousness raising," where we link individual experiences to patterns of oppression across society (Sarachild, 1970). As long as we remain focused on incidents, we see the plight of individual women as indicators that otherwise functional family or community systems require some readjustment (Goodrich et al., 1988). From this viewpoint, the violence is minimized as normal malfunctions. Through consciousness raising, people are supported and challenged to rethink the causes of shared experiences such as male jealousy and female dependency and to identify their common roots in social expectations such as unilateral caregiving by women.

The third step in countering women abuse is to integrate our understanding of women abuse with our actions to stop it. Without such an integration, we simply react to incidents of abuse and attend to various aspects of the violence but not its totality. The result is a fragmented system of human service delivery in which one agency or program protects children against parental abuse and neglect, another offers counselling to abuse survivors, another incarcerates the perpetrators, another treats the physical injuries, another medicates the resulting mental health problems. The difficulty is not the range of programs but rather their narrow focus, which can blind them to the prevalence and systemic nature of women abuse. If the social worker sees only the mother's depression, the assessment is likely to focus on her personality rather than the possibility that she may be reacting to violence. If the doctor sees only minor, ill-defined pains, the diagnosis is likely to reflect the view that the woman is immature and complaining rather than suffering from abuse.

Guided by an expanded awareness of the social basis of abuse, we do not react to incidents of abuse but instead engage in reflective action. We see people as embedded in their families and communities and work to build an understanding and strategy that addresses human lives as a whole. In so doing, we set up a process by which we continually learn through open discussion, raising consciousness and reflecting on what we are doing together.

Dialogue

The social work literature did not refer to family violence until the latter half of the 1960s (Elbow, 1980). Such silence may appear astounding especially given the profession's early and continuing involvement in women abuse. In her study of records of child welfare agencies in Boston, Linda Gordon (1988) discovered that at the turn of the century many women workers responded to the pleas of mothers for protection from their abusive partners. During the nineteenth century in Canada, male violence was identified as a concern by moral reformers and social workers. The temperance movement connected male drunkenness with domestic violence and poverty (Duley, 1993), and philanthropists and their successors, social workers, identified incest although exclusively as a problem in working-class homes (Valverde, 1991). While the moral imperialism of these social reformers has been repeatedly highlighted, their efforts to counter women and child abuse and other social problems and to advance the rights of women have been obscured.

Beginning in the late 1960s, the second-wave feminist movement redirected attention to the oppression of women. Women speaking with other women about their experiences told stories of tyranny manifested through such diverse embodiments as domestic obligations, professional diagnoses, social welfare criteria, academic canons and romantic appeals. Understanding of women's lives broadened as attention was given to the voices of women of colour, old women, disabled women, rural women, lesbian women, poor and working-class women and women who combine these and other circumstances and life choices. These stories revealed how girls are not only socialized to care but also are "policed to care" through social ostracism, the threat or use of physical force by male intimates, and the authority of legal and human service institutions (Reitsma-Street, 1991).

The breaking of the silence led to recharacterization of actions previously typed by professionals as "family conflict" or "sexual aggression" into politically charged terms — "rape," "wife assault" and "battered women" — that exposed both the violence and the gender of its victims. The renaming made it possible to identify and count instances. In 1980, reporting the research of Linda MacLeod, the Canadian Advisory Council on the Status of Women was able to present the first national estimate of women battering. At the time, the figure of one in ten women being battered by her partner startled the Canadian public. Today, the reported figures are far higher. Statistics Canada's (1993) *Violence Against Women Survey* found that one out of four women had experienced physical or sexual violence by a marital or common-law partner. This finding not only reveals the wide-spread prevalence of violence in Canadian society but also the ability of women to name their experiences. It is important to note that before Statistics Canada undertook this survey, its representatives consulted with shelter staff, rape crisis counsellors and others on how to interview women so as not to endanger their safety and privacy and to create the conditions within which women could tell their stories.

Counting has also made it possible to compare the experiences of men and women. Although women are known to abuse male and female partners, men are the perpetrators in far greater numbers. Canadian crime statistics show that men and women are equally likely to be the reported victims of violent crimes, but that the spouse or ex-spouse was accused in 43 per cent of violent crimes against women while the percentage was only three per cent in the case of male victims (Trevethan and Tajeshwer, 1992). Crime statistics also show that a woman is three times more likely to be killed by her husband than a man by his wife (Wilson and Daly, 1994). Initially, however, there were reports of near equal rates of violence by husbands and wives (Straus, Gelles and Steinmetz, 1980), but these findings were quickly challenged on methodological and common sense grounds (Berk et al., 1983). People knew that a slap by most women in no way equalled those by their male partners in force and injury. Listening to accounts of abuse, counsellors and researchers learned that the motivations for the violence tended to differ: typically men, despite excuses of being out of control, were exerting control (Ptacek, 1988) while women were often trying to defend themselves or their children (Saunders, 1988).

Sensitive listening to women's stories is helping us to identify the interconnections between women and child abuse. Commonly child welfare workers become involved at a time when mothers are not coping with their children or their own lives. The tendency is to blame mothers and apprehend children rather than identifying the poverty and violence that they have endured (Callahan, 1993). Although women provide most of the care for children, we are increasingly recognizing that men perpetuate not only the vast majority of child sexual abuse but also a sizable portion of the physical abuse. One U.S. study found that 70 per cent of the wife beaters also physically abused their children (Bowker, Arbitell and McFerron, 1988); and another one found that almost two-thirds of abused children had mothers who were also being battered (Stark and Flitcraft, 1988).

The reasons for the violence against the children and young people vary (McKay, 1994). Sometimes the children become accidental victims when the partner attacks their mother, or fathers retaliate against adolescent sons trying to protect their mothers; other times the mothers may over discipline the children in an attempt to ward off outbreaks of violence by her partner; and yet other times the mother may be so beaten down that she withdraws from or abuses her children. Whether or not the children are the direct recipients of the violence, they suffer extensive pain from witnessing the abuse of their mothers.

Critical Analysis

Countering women abuse has enriched our knowledge but also poses its own risks. These risks, though, can be avoided by intensifying the dialogue through critical analysis. We can engage in critical analysis when we have an alternative standpoint from which to re-examine our ideas. The feminist movement offers such a vantage point in helping us to rethink the meaning of abuse.

One risk from countering comes from numeration itself, which leads to adding up people according to categories. Even when the results are so large as those reported by the 1993 Statistics Canada survey, they still can leave the impression that abuse happens to certain unfortunate women and not to others. The analysis then narrows to the characteristics or situations of individual victims and perpetrators rather than widening to recognize the pervasiveness of women abuse throughout Canadian society. Although numerous studies reveal variations in the proportion of women abuse for people from different age groups, socioeconomic statuses and backgrounds (Stark and Flitcraft, 1991), the consistent finding is that within industrialized societies women are abused in all populations. For instance, although Canadian women with the lowest incomes (below $15,000) have the highest rate of physical and sexual assault by partners and others (13 per cent), the percentage of difference between them and the least violated group of women (incomes between $30,000-$59,999) is only four percentage points apart (Statistics Canada, 1993). Moreover, it is quite likely that the differences between income groups would disappear if poor women received the same level of police protection as women with higher incomes.

Another, equally dangerous risk of countering is that high statistics can be used to justify the theory that violence is natural to the male half of the human species, and, thus, is unavoidable or at best somewhat containable. Such an interpretation overlooks counterevidence that not all cultures have been historically rife with women abuse (Masumura, 1979). Universalizing women abuse is reinforced by the tendency to conduct surveys of violence in industrialized regions and to ignore other types of societies. While commendable in many ways, Statistics Canada's *Survey on Violence Against Women* is in all likelihood biased away from alternative cultures within Canada because it was conducted by telephone and only in English or French. Interestingly, this same survey found that Newfoundland and Labrador, one of the more traditional regions of Canada, had a substantially lower reported rate of women abuse than any other province.

To understand women abuse, social workers must look beyond statistics to identifying the social structures and norms that permit it, the social networks that entrap women and the choices that people make to survive. Social workers often assess the probability or risk of abuse on the basis of personal qualities such as substance abuse, high stress and violence in family of origin. While these characteristics are frequently associated with violence, our analysis becomes skewed when we confuse the causes of abuse with its outcomes or contexts. For example, battered women are more likely to have an alcohol problem than nonbattered women, but this appears to be a consequence rather than antecedent of abuse; battering men are more likely to drink excessively than nonbattering men, but when they stop drinking their abusiveness persists (Stark and Flitcraft, 1991). Rather than accusing women who drink of "asking for it," we should consider why they do not receive the help that they need to stop the abuse and, as a result, they turn to alcohol to suppress the pain. And rather than accepting that "he was drunk," we should consider why societal norms rationalize violence by men who are intoxicated.

Another danger of emphasizing statistical differences is that we can attribute too much influence to certain experiences and, therefore, minimize people's resilience and capacity for choice. A prime example is a currently popular theory called the Intergenerational Cycle of Violence. This social learning theory posits that childhood experiences of abuse will make the individual more susceptible to entering abusive relationships as an adult. In support of this theory, the violence against women survey (Rodgers, 1994) found that men whose fathers were violent were three times more likely than men whose fathers were not violent to abuse their current partner; women whose fathers had been violent were twice as likely as women whose fathers had not been violent to be abused by their current partner. The same survey, however, also found that both men and women from homes with violent fathers were now far more often in nonviolent relationships. Interestingly, a study of 84 homeless women in Toronto reports that the majority of these women were assaulted prior to leaving home, usually by a father or stepfather, but once they left home, in almost all cases, these women, who would appear to be in quite vulnerable circumstances, evaded further abuse by either male partners or boyfriends (Breton and Bunston, 1992).

As social workers, we need to consider the consequences of early abuse on later relationships but should not take its effects as given. Otherwise, we and those with whom we work will become pessimistic about the future of countless children. We need to broaden our analysis to consider the resources that our communities offer children to help them adopt nonviolence. What are the existing cooperative practices? What are the traditions that emphasize the spiritual equality of men and women? We need to deepen our analysis to consider the context of relationships within which the violence transpired (Jaffe, Wolfe and Wilson, 1990). Was the child buffered from lowered self-esteem by the presence of a caring adult? How was the child able to distance herself or himself from the abuser? And we need to validate the capacity of people to choose not to replicate aspects of their histories that they reject.

Unified Action

Unified action is a collaborative effort to address a common concern. Such an approach is essential for countering women abuse, which requires a total recasting of male-dominant relationships into a mutually caring form. This remolding can not be carried out by one group on its own; it necessitates co-operative redesigning. A review of the history of the shelter movement in Canada shows how progress was initially achieved through the efforts of women's organizations and how they exerted pressure to involve state institutions. Without structures in place to promote unified action, however, state involvement can lead not to cooperation but instead to cooptation with change efforts reabsorbed into existing practices of encountering women abuse (see Walker, 1990). The question then posed is: How can such a seemingly visionary approach be adopted so that families, communities and state institutions can work together?

Prior to the 1970s, a scattering of religious or philanthropic organizations provided some temporary refuge to homeless women, including abused women, but with social service agencies notably absent from these efforts (Gilman, 1988). The take-off of shelters did not occur until women, based in feminist, religious and grass-roots groups, took unilateral action to offer safe places by opening their homes or their women's centres and building safety networks for women fleeing from violence (Beaudry, 1985). Out of these efforts grew the shelter movement with 376 transition houses in Canada by 1992 (MacDonald and Touchette, 1993). Over the past two decades, shelters have extended their programs beyond emergency housing to providing a wider range of counselling, advocacy and follow-up services to their residents, adult and child; and new shelters have been opened to reach women in rural and remote areas and women from diverse cultures. Despite these advances, there is much room for shelters to address the needs of nonmainstream women such as those who are disabled and recent immigrants to Canada.

Shelter activists realized, though, that they alone could not protect abused women and their children; they needed to move "beyond the shelter doors" and make connections with other organizations in order to engage in social change work (Blackbear, 1991). They pushed law enforcement, social service and health institutions and increasingly businesses to take action. This strategy has been effective in securing material and legal resources for battered women and their children. For instance, mothers who are homeless because of violence are often placed as a priority on the waiting lists for public housing.

Involving state institutions, however, has had mixed results, as particularly evident in the case of law enforcement agencies. Measures to have spouse assault treated as any other violent crime have, on the one hand, served to advance the position that such mistreatment is criminal; they have, on the other hand, offered only limited protection to women. Criminal law covers only physical and sexual assault and, thus, ignores the very detrimental effect of emotional abuse. Moreover, punishment of offenders has not been as effective as originally anticipated. Contrary to initial findings, recent studies of the impact of arrest on spouse abusers have not shown this to be a better deterrent to recidivism than less punitive strategies such as the police issuing a citation or temporarily separating a couple (Hirschel and Hutchison, 1992).

Abused women recount numerous stories of revictimization at the hands of the police and courts (Nichols, 1991). Although many workers within the justice system are well intentioned, the adversarial nature of the legal system forces women to testify against men for whom they may still care, from whom they fear retaliation and upon whom they may depend financially (MacLeod, 1990). Many of these women want the police and the judges to affirm that their partner was in the wrong, but they also do not want to be placed under an obligation to testify against him if they are to receive any support through the courts.

Crown prosecutors, frustrated by the reluctance of abused women to give evidence against their partners, pressed for contempt charges to compel victims to serve as witnesses. They quickly learned that the spectacle of the abused woman being imprisoned for failing to give testimony rather than her assailant provokes public outrage. Another route utilized by public prosecutions in Saskatchewan is giving abused women the information and support to think over what they want to do, such preparation has been found to circumvent the necessity of coercing victims into testifying (McGillivray, 1987). This alternative, while helpful for some women, makes it possible to treat the abused woman as a special case rather than acknowledging the necessity of reworking the legal system.

The experience with the legal system reveals that responsibility for controlling perpetrators can not simply be handed over to the police and courts. It is a formal way of holding offenders accountable for their actions, but it is not designed to attend to the needs and hopes of those who have been victimized. The Canadian justice system is based on a liberal ideology of individualism in which the defendant and victim are viewed as two distinct parties rather than as a couple with numerous ties. The answer to this conundrum, however, does not lie in abandoning the legal or other state routes for addressing woman abuse but instead in developing a unified strategy.

Principles for Countering Women Abuse

Three principles are presented for countering women abuse. They are guidelines on how to carry out the feminist teachings to make it possible for people to tell their stories, to develop a critical analysis, and to develop a unified strategy. To be effective these principles need to be applied in unison rather than separately. The principles are based upon the author's experiences within the battered women's movement (Pennell, 1990), with alliances across progressive social movements (Pennell, 1993) and in partnerships among families, communities and government departments (Pennell and Burford, in-press). These experiences have shown that it is possible to create a system of mutual caring in which people have a voice over their affairs and the resources and protections to make this possible. They have also shown that there is no one route for achieving this objective and that each one must be fashioned within the culture of the particular family, organization or community.

Building Communal Supports

The first principle is building the supportive networks that nurture and safeguard. It cannot be assumed that these will emerge spontaneously from families and their communities. If they did, women and child abuse would not be so prevalent across Canadian society. Many community values and practices have sustained women and child abuse, but we can also reach out for alternative perspectives from within a culture and promote dialogue between cultures so that they can learn from each other. Canadians of European descent are learning much from First Nation's peoples about community-based approaches to stopping violence and healing survivors and perpetrators. At the same time, white people need to identify their own cultural diversity and traditions of collective caring. Supports can be built by reconnecting people with their kin, neighbours, co-workers and by severing or monitoring connections that threaten the person's well-being. These steps need to be undertaken with people's consent and participation and with particular attention to the wishes of those who have been abused.

Having a Say

The second principle is creating contexts in which all family members have a say over how they choose to live together or apart from each other. While this principle would need to be adjusted in accordance with a child's age and maturity, the aim is to promote decision making in which the views of all family members are taken seriously and incorporated into plans. Carrying out such decision making does not require that participants be exceptionally verbal or intelligent. It does require disclosing experiences and opinions in safety and reaching out for the views of others. It also requires that outsiders do not block this process and that they support the enactment of reasonable decisions.

Ensuring Resources and Protections

In a male-dominant society, power within families has been skewed away from participatory decision making. For all family members to exert a real voice over their lives, external intervention may be essential. Community organizations and public authorities have a responsibility to provide, where necessary, material resources and protective measures. Equally importantly, they need to project a firm stance that no one should be abused and everyone has a responsibility for caring.

Reassessing Social Work Practice

These three principles for countering woman abuse challenge us as social workers to clarify our role, not an easy task given the conflicting expectations laid upon us. Legislation, agency policies and public demands simultaneously push us to stop family violence, respect the privacy of families and minimize expenditures in meeting their needs. As a profession, we are committed to advancing our clients' self-determination while at the same time we have the responsibility to intervene when necessitated by life-threatening circumstances and choices. The result is that we feel pressured to find immediate solutions rather than working with others to develop them.

If we are to move beyond encountering to countering women abuse, we need to reappraise how social workers are responding to violence. We cannot undertake this self-assessment without the collaboration of others dedicated to ending the abuse and without our faith in the worth of all people, male and female, renewed by alternative perspectives. To reassess our interventions against women abuse, we must start by listening to the stories of those whom we are seeking to help. Without such knowledge we remain uninformed of their experiences of the abuse and the effects of the response, or its lack, to the violence. To hear their stories, we need to develop the conditions and relationships that foster safe disclosure. Within this context, participants can engage in full and honest discussion, draw upon the insights and inventiveness of the group, and make informed decisions on how to work together to halt the violence. At the same time as we strive to end women abuse, we collectively reflect on the merits and demerits of our approaches and reshape them as our understanding grows.

References

Abramovitz, M. 1988. *Regulating the Lives of Women: Social Welfare Policy From Colonial Times to the Present.* Boston: South End Press.

Baines, C. T., Evans, P. M. and Neysmith, S. M. (eds.). 1991. *Women's Caring: Feminist Perspectives on Social Welfare.* Toronto: McClelland and Stewart.

Beaudry, M. 1985. *Battered Women* (L. Huston and M. Heap, Trans.). Montreal: Black Rose.

Berk, R. A., Berk, S. F., Loseke, D. R. and Rauma, D. 1983. "Mutual Combat and Other Family Violence Myths," in Finkelhor, D., R. J. Gelles, G. T. Hotaling and M. A. Straus (eds.), *The Dark Side of Families: Current Family Violence Research.* Beverly Hills: Sage, pp. 197-212.

Blackbear, T. 1991. "Beyond the Shelter Doors: Making the Connections." In conference proceedings, *Alternatives: Directions in the Nineties to End the Abuse of Women.* Winnipeg, Manitoba: Educational Committee Against the Abuse of Women (Manitoba) Inc., pp. 20-34.

Bowker, L. H., Arbitell, M. and McFerron, J. R. 1988. "On the Relationship Between Wife Beating and Child Abuse," in K. Yllö and M. Bograd, (eds.), *Feminist Perspectives on Wife Abuse.* Newbury Park: Sage, pp. 158-174.

Breton, M. and Bunston, T. 1992. "Physical and Sexual Violence in the Lives of Homeless Women." *Canadian Journal of Community Mental Health.* 11: 29-44.

Butler, S. 1985. *Conspiracy of Silence: The Trauma of Incest.* San Francisco: Volcano Press.

Callahan, M. 1993. "Feminist Approaches: Women Recreate Child Welfare," in Wharf, B. (ed.), *Rethinking Child Welfare in Canada.* Toronto: McClelland and Stewart, pp. 172-209.

Duley, M. I. 1993. *Where Once Our Mothers Stood We Stand: Women's Suffrage in Newfoundland 1890-1925.* Charlottetown: Gynergy Books.

Elbow, M. (ed.). 1980. *Patterns in Family Violence.* New York: Family Service Association of America.

Gilman, S. T. 1988. "A History of the Sheltering Movement For Battered Women in Canada." *Canadian Journal of Community Mental Health.* 7: 2, 9-21.

Goodrich, T. J., Rampage, C., Ellman, B. and Halstead, K. 1988. *Feminist Family Therapy: A Casebook.* New York: W. W. Norton.

Gordon, L. 1988. *Heroes of Their Own Lives: The Politics and History of Family Violence.* New York: Viking.

Hirschel, J. D. and Hutchison, III, I. W. 1992. "Female Spouse Abuse and the Police Response: The Charlotte, North Carolina Experiment." *Journal of Criminal Law and Criminology.* 83: 1, 73-119.

Hodgson, M. and Client: "Phyllis." 1990. In T. A. Laidlaw, C. Malmo, and Associates, *Healing Voices: Feminist Approaches to Therapy With Women.* San Francisco: Jossey-Bass, pp. 33-44.

Hoff, L. A. 1990. *Battered Women as Survivors.* New York: Routledge.

Jaffe, P. G., Wolfe, D. A. and Wilson, S. K. 1990. *Children of Battered Women.* Newbury Park, CA: Sage.

Luxton, M., Rosenberg, H. and Arat Koç, S. (eds.). 1990. *Through the Kitchen Window: The Politics of Home and Family,* 2nd edition. Toronto: Garamond Press.

MacDonald, G. and Touchette, L. 1993. "Profile of Transition Homes/Shelters For Victims of Family Violence." *Health Reports,* 5: 2, Statistics Canada Cat. No. 82-003.

MacLeod, L. 1980. *Wife Battering in Canada: The Vicious Circle*. Ottawa: Canadian Advisory Council on the Status of Women.

MacLeod, L. 1990. *Sharing the Responsibility for Justice*. A speech presented at the Provincial Symposium on Woman Abuse and the Criminal Justice System, Moncton, New Brunswick.

Mahoney, M. R. 1991. "Legal Images of Battered Women: Redefining the Issue of Separation." *Michigan Law Review*. 90: 1.

Marchant, H. 1986. "Gender, Systems Thinking and Radical Social Work," in Marchant H. and B. Wearing (eds.), *Gender Reclaimed: Women in Social Work*. Sydney: Hale and Iremonger, pp. 14-32.

Masumura, W. T. 1979. "Wife Abuse and Other Forms of Aggression." *Victimology: An International Journal*. 4: 1, 46-59.

Maynard, M. 1985. "The Response of Social Workers to Domestic Violence," in Pahl, J. (ed.), *Private Violence and Public Policy: The Needs of Battered Women and the Response of the Public Services*. London: Routledge and Kegan Paul.

McGillivray, A. 1987. "Battered Women: Definition, Models and Prosecutorial Policy." *Canadian Journal of Family Law*. 6: 16-45.

McKay, M. M. 1994. "The Link Between Domestic Violence and Child Abuse: Assessment and Treatment Considerations." *Child Welfare*. 73: 1, 29-39.

Nichols, A. 1991. "Whose Rights Are Wronged? The N.W.T. Faces a Change in the Way Its Legal System Treats Women." *Northernher: North America's First Circumpolar Women's Magazine*. 1: 1, 7-9.

Pennell, J. 1990. "Democratic Hierarchy in Feminist Organizations." *Dissertation Abstracts International*. 50/12-A, 4118. (University Microfilms No. AAD90-15034).

Pennell, J. 1993. "Should Shelter Staff Unionize?" *Perception*. 17: 3, 25-27.

Pennell, J. and Burford, G. (in-press). "Widening the Circle: The Family Group Decision Making Project." *Journal of Child and Youth Care*. 9: 1.

Pilowsky, J. E. 1993. "The Courage to Leave: An Exploration of Spanish-speaking Women Victims of Spousal Abuse." *Canadian Journal of Community Mental Health*. 12: 2, 15-29.

Ptacek, J. 1988. "Why Do Men Batter Their Wives?" in Yllö, K. and M. Bograd (eds.), *Feminist perspectives on wife abuse*. Newbury Park: Sage, pp. 133-157.

Reitsma-Street, M. 1991. "Girls Learn to Care; Girls Policed to Care," in Baines, C. T., P. M. Evans and S. M. Neysmith (eds.), *Women's Caring: Feminist Perspectives on Social Welfare*. Toronto: McClelland and Stewart, pp. 106-137.

Rodgers, K. 1994. "Wife Assault: The Findings of a National Survey." *Juristat Service Bulletin*. 14: 9, Statistics Canada Cat. No. 85-002.

Sarachild, K. 1970. "Feminist Consciousness Raising and `Organizing'." in Tanner, L. B. (ed.), *Voices From Women's Liberation*. New York: New American Library, pp. 154-157.

Saunders, D. G. 1988. "Wife Abuse, Husband Abuse, or Mutual Combat? A Feminist Perspective on the Empirical Findings," in Yllö, K. and M. Bograd (eds.), *Feminist Perspectives on Wife Abuse*. Newbury Park: Sage, pp. 90-113.

Segal, L. 1990. *Slow Motion: Changing Masculinities, Changing Men*. New Brunswick, NJ: Rutgers University Press.

Sinclair, P. R. and Felt, L. F. 1992. "Separate Worlds: Gender and Domestic Labour in an Isolated Fishing Region." *Canadian Review of Sociology and Anthropology*. 29:1, 55-71.

Stark, E. and Flitcraft, A. 1988. "Women and Children at Risk: A Feminist Perspective on Child Abuse." *International Journal of Health Services*. 18: 1, 97-118.

Stark, E. and Flitcraft, A. 1991. "Spouse Abuse," in Rosenberg, M. L. and M. A. Fenley (eds.), *Violence in America: A Public Health Approach*. New York: Oxford University Press, pp. 121-157.

Statistics Canada. 1993. "The Violence Against Women Survey: Highlights." *The Daily*, Cat. No. 11-001E.

Straus, M.A., Gelles, R. J. and Steinmetz, S. K. 1980. *Behind Closed Doors: Violence in the American Family*. New York: Doubleday/Anchor.

Swift, K. 1991. "Contradictions in Child Welfare: Neglect and Responsibility," in Baines, C. T., P. M. Evans and S. M. Neysmith (eds.), *Women's Caring: Feminist Perspectives on Social Welfare*. Toronto: McClelland and Stewart, pp. 234-271.

Trevethan, S. and Tajeshwer, S. 1992. "Gender Differences Among Victims of Violent Crime." *Juristat Service Bulletin*. 12: 21, Statistics Canada Cat. No. 85-002.

Ursel, J. 1992. *Private Lives, Public Policy: 100 Years of State Intervention Into the Family*. Toronto: Women's Press.

Valverade, M. 1991. *The Age of Light, Soap, and Water: Moral Reform in English Canada 1885-1925*. Toronto: McClelland and Stewart.

Walker, G. A. 1990. *Family Violence and the Women's Movement: The Conceptual Politics of Struggle*. Toronto: University of Toronto Press.

Wilson, M. and Daly, M. 1994. "Spousal Homicide." *Juristat Service Bulletin*. 14: 8, Statistics Canada Cat. No. 85-002.

Chapter VII
Gender and Occupational Closure in Social Work

Leslie Bella

Professionalization is about power rather than about protecting the public interest by ensuring service quality. Professionalization involves a process of occupational closure intended to limit the supply of entrants to an occupation. This chapter shows that recent registration initiatives of Canada's provincial social work associations have used strategies of exclusion, segregation and subordination to achieve occupational closure. These strategies may result in deskilling and heightened interprofessional competition. Implications for social work education and for professional discipline are outlined.

Although professional ideologies claim that professionalization is self-evidently in the public interest, professionalization is really about power as much as service quality or protection of the public (Johnson, 1972; Wilding, 1982; Hamowy, 1984; Witz, 1992). While professional organizations do sometimes use their power toward the public good (Bella, 1991), professionalization is actually a process of occupational closure designed to limit and control the supply of entrants to an occupation, and thereby enhance their market value (Parkin, 1979; Witz, 1992, p. 41). Occupational groups achieve closure through legislation (requiring state cooperation), and through credentials (requiring cooperation with educational institutions). This closure can be achieved by excluding a group from the occupation (exclusion), by admitting the group to the profession but to less prestigious and lucrative roles (segregation) and by a relationship through which one occupational group controls the work of another (subordination).

The occupational groups who began to professionalize in the Victorian era, and have their roots in entrepreneurial and autonomous practice, tended to be male dominated, as was Victorian medicine and law (Friedson, 1970; Larson, 1977). Many of the newer occupations, like nursing, social work and teaching, are female dominated and have pursued professionalization in relation to employment in caring roles within state funded bureaucracies (Baines, 1991). These newer occupations are described by some as "semi-professions" (Etzioni, 1969) because they do not follow the same model as the male-dominated, entrepreneurial occupations of the nineteenth century. However, even the older professions now work less autonomously. For example, Canadian physicians practice within the framework of medicare, hospital administration, group practice and private insurance and their individual autonomy is limited (Coburn, Torrance and Kaufer, 1983).

With men predominant in some occupational groups and women in others, the processes of professionalization are also gendered (Witz, 1992). For example, the male-dominated medical profession used all three strategies of occupational closure against women. With the cooperation of universities and teaching hospitals they excluded women from membership. The Victorian medical profession also struggled to exclude midwives from caring for women in childbirth (Ehrenreich and English, 1973; Hamowy, 1984). They eventually agreed to occupational segregation with male physicians serving wealthier patients and midwives working with poorer families. After medicare, midwives were further restricted to work in remote rural areas not served by physicians. Medicine also sought to subordinate midwifery by defining educational requirements, identifying "normal" deliveries that could be safely attended by midwives and limiting midwives to helping women before and after birth but not at the moment of birth itself. The medical profession also subordinated the occupation of nursing, participating in the design of education and training of female workers whose primary role would be to carry out physicians' orders (Keddy et al., 1986). The medical profession has also attempted occupational closure in relation to other male-dominated professions such as chiropractic (Coburn and Biggs, 1986). Concomitantly, nurses (Warrington-Turcke, 1983; Melosh, 1989) and midwives have also pursued occupational closure, against both male- and female-dominated occupational groups.

A gendered pattern has also emerged within occupational groups that include both men and women. Men find their way into the more prestigious, lucrative and technically complex roles, and women into generalized roles in more poorly paid positions requiring less technical expertise and more of the undervalued caring abilities stereotypically expected of women. This internal gender specialization within a profession has also been demonstrated in radiography (Witz, 1992) and law as well as social work.

Social work began as a female-dominated occupation, but now tends to include a significant and influential minority of men. The occupation developed in the work of middle- and upper-middle class Victorian women, serving as volunteers in charity organization societies and settlement houses. The female occupation of social work first began to professionalize by developing education programs and credentialling. Mary Richmond embodied the aspiring profession's claim to specialized knowledge in *Social Diagnosis* (1917), an American text using medical concepts of diagnosis and treatment to frame a "scientific" approach to social work. Thus, an occupation born in the caring work of women used the technical and scientific language of medical men. Social work education programs were introduced in Canadian universities, first in Toronto (Hurl, 1983) and then at McGill. These schools were usually led by male social scientists, often without social work practice experience but with academic credentials acceptable to the university. These men usually taught social work theory, research, administration, corrections and policy courses, while women with experience as social workers taught practice courses in areas such as families, children, health care and the elderly. Thus, in its first attempts at professionalization Canadian social work used concepts derived from the science of the dominant and masculine health profession, and also positioned men in social work education to define the nature of social work and to develop its knowledge and theory base. Already, professionalization in social work was sought through masculinization.

While men had elite positions in social work education, the occupation of social work in Canada remained predominantly a women's domain. When members of the aspiring profession became concerned at the low status of their occupation in the 1930s, they sought to correct this by recruiting men into the profession. Recruiting pamphlets in both the Toronto school and the Canadian Association of Social Workers (CASW) stressed the need for men in social work. One 1938 pamphlet suggested that men would be most appropriate for work with boys in corrections and in relief administration. Women could work with children and families and in medical social work. Men were subsequently attracted to social service work, but were less likely than women to be trained and more likely to be in administrative positions. Men, like fathers, were assumed to have the firmness and consistency to administer and correct, regardless of their training (Struthers, 1987). Women, like stereotypic mothers, were sought for their ability to care and nurture. This gendered pattern, with men predominant in administration and women in front line work, persists in social work today (Bella, 1992).

Social work, like other occupations, is concerned with occupational closure and has used both legislation and credentials to exclude, to segregate and to subordinate. Some social workers believe that strategies of occupational closure are inconsistent with social work's democratic, egalitarian and predominantly "welfare liberal" values (Bella, 1991). They challenge the call for higher educational standards for the profession, saying these are detrimental to women and to marginalized groups such as native people, immigrants and others serving in multicultural agencies. If social work regulation resulted in exclusion of minorities from the profession, then this was inconsistent with the profession's Code of Ethics (Alcock, 1990). Recent initiatives toward self-regulation in social work as described below clearly demonstrate the tension between demands for occupational closure on the one hand and the egalitarian and liberal values expressed in the profession's Code of Ethics on the other.

Social work regulation has taken several forms. First, registration can be entrenched in provincial legislation (as is now the case in most provinces) or can be a voluntary initiative of the provincial association without status in law. Ontario is now the only province without legislated social work registration, but it has its own form of voluntary self-regulation. Second, registration is usually required of all those who wish to use the title social worker, or in some province the title R.S.W. (registered social worker) or C.S.W. (certified social worker). This is known as "protection of title" or "certification" (Maton, 1988). In some provinces, such as Newfoundland, registration legislation also permits only registered social workers to practice social work. This is known as "control of practice" and constitutes licensure rather than certification. Finally, registration can be compulsory or required only for certain groups of social workers, such as private practitioners, or completely voluntary. Social work will have attained full occupational closure when legislation provides for compulsory registration, control of title, control of practice and specifies educational credentials for admission.

Canada's social work associations have been struggling for self-regulation for more than 60 years (Gowanlock, 1986). This process has accelerated over the last five years. In 1988, all provinces but Prince Edward Island and Ontario had legislation regulating social work practice (Maton, 1988; Gowanlock, 1990), but only Prince Edward Island had full compulsory registration of social workers. In 1989, the CASW board reviewed an assessment of this situation (Bella, 1989; Landry, 1990), and after internal debate its journal published a status report (Walsh, 1990a, 1990b). In spite of Alcock's warnings about the inconsistency between occupational closure and the profession's democratic values, commitment to professionalization was renewed in the provinces outside Quebec (Landry, 1990). Over the next few years all the anglophone provincial associations worked to increase professionalization.[1] They created committees, drafted legislative proposals and lobbied provincial governments for strengthened social work registration legislation.

By the end of 1993, new social work legislation had been introduced in British Columbia, Alberta, Saskatchewan, New Brunswick and Newfoundland. This represents a significant move toward professionalization and what Witz would describe as a successful "female professional project" (1992, p. 208). As is shown below, Canadian social work's contemporary attempts to achieve compulsory registration, control of title and control of practice reflects both the internal gendered structure of the profession and the profession's relationships to other male- and female-dominated occupations at various stages of professionalization.

These initiatives are outlined below, and implications for the gendered nature of the profession, and of the profession's relationships with other social groups such as public sector managers, paraprofessionals, clients and client advocates.

Social Work Registration Initiatives in Canada's Provinces

Newfoundland had legislation providing for voluntary registration in 1979. However, the provincial government delayed implementation, setting up a committee to prepare regulations but not accepting its recommendations. By 1987 the province had still not responded:

> The struggle for registration continues. In recent discussions the Minister of Social Services made a commitment to discuss NASW's position with Cabinet. He is hopeful there can be a satisfactory resolution within the next few months. (*The Social Worker*, 1987, 55: 4, 187)

The province continued to stall until the disclosures of sexual abuse at the Mount Cashel orphanage allowed the National Association of Social Workers (NASW) to highlight the need for social work registration. Survivors' testimony before the Hughes Inquiry of 1989-1990 drew the public eye both to the abuse and to the lack of response by the province's public agencies. Police and social services had evidently been impeded or obstructed, and complaints and allegations had been suppressed. The Roman Catholic Church, the police and the Department of Social Services were all implicated. The NASW used this opportunity to bring all their organizational resources to focus on registration. In their brief to the Hughes Commission the association argued that the real problem at Mount Cashel was the lack of professional education and status for social workers. NASW argued that:

1. Many of the persons responsible for social work service to complainants did not have the benefit of professional education;

2. Professional social workers did not have the support of an influential licensing body that could provide a strong point of reference for the applications of standards of ethical practice and standards of social work care. (Kimberly and Rowe, 1991a)

The NASW brief argued that the government of Newfoundland was responsible for what happened at Mount Cashel, for "despite the pleas of our association, it had left it until this crisis to seriously consider effective legislation to control title and practice" (Kimberly and Rowe, 1991a). The association asked for new legislation, rather than for implementation of the existing ten-year-old act, arguing that social workers needed "a strong reference point outside of the employing organizations," to prevent them succumbing to "organizational and self-interest."

This argument was ultimately effective, and in 1993 new legislation gave the new Newfoundland Association of Social Workers control over both the title "social worker" and over the practice of social work. However, the arguments used by NASW are seen by some Newfoundland social workers as self-serving and as a betrayal of those who tried to serve the young people at Mount Cashel. The NASW brief had explicitly blamed social workers, primarily women, for what went wrong at Mount Cashel. The real culprits, the abusers themselves and the ministers, senior bureaucrats, church officials and senior police officers — all male — are invisible in the NASW brief, except that they would presumably all have been brought to account if social workers had just been more professional.

With legislation requiring registration and controlling both title and practice, Newfoundland's social workers appear to have attained occupational closure. However, this success is to some extent illusory. The majority of the managers of the province's own social workers are men, many of them without social work credentials. While the line workers themselves will have to be registered, managers will not. Hence, while the legislation provides "closure" in terms of line positions, it comes at the cost of subordination to a class of male public managers who are not expected to be social workers.

The Newfoundland legislation also ensures that, with a few exceptions grandfathered in shortly following the passage of legislation, all those in social work positions will have to complete a B.S.W. in order to be registered. This effective occupational closure may cause hardship for those currently working in social work positions with a B.A. rather than a B.S.W. These workers, predominantly women, have been hired into temporary positions. The provincial government has shown no commitment to helping these workers upgrade, preferring to lay them off and hire fresh graduates. Restricted enrolment at Memorial's School of Social Work, particularly in the second degree program, has prevented them from upgrading and they are vulnerable to lay off when new B.S.W.s graduate.

The new social work registration provisions are also problematic for the province's social work services in Labrador. The provincial department has realized that the indigenous people of Labrador, both Inuit and Innu, are best served by people who understand their culture and who preferably share their language and cultural background. As a result, indigenous community service workers work under the supervision of qualified white social workers. While some community service workers have university educations and may take advantage of grandfathering, none have social work credentials and some would not meet even the minimum requirements for admission to Memorial University. Without the credentials for registration, the community service workers are a subordinated occupational group needing supervision by white social workers before they can legally provide child welfare and other social work services to their own people. Both aboriginal social work education and aboriginal social agencies will be required before aboriginal social workers can work autonomously. The Newfoundland example shows that, as suggested by Alcock, occupational closure can act against the interests of minorities.

Social workers in Nova Scotia had worked since 1963 under legislation providing for voluntary legislation (Gowanlock, 1986). However, in 1985 the need for "substantial amendment" led the association to create a public regulation committee to study legislation in other provinces and in the United States. Legislative proposals were drafted requiring mandatory registration and retaining existing standards for entry to the profession. The Nova Scotia Association of Social Workers (NSASW) hoped this would strengthen the profession:

> The increasing tendency among employers to down-scale entry qualifications for social work positions, the loss of ground to adjacent professions, and the lack of an effective voice in the social action/policy arena all attest to the need for a strong, unified professional association.

In October 1987, the association approved these proposals. The province, however, did not introduce new social work legislation, and by 1993 the association was still seeking agreement with the provincial government on new legislation.

In 1965, the New Brunswick Association of Social Workers (NBASW) was incorporated in New Brunswick legislation. In the 1980s, the association reviewed legislation providing mandatory registration elsewhere. In 1987, the association "renewed support" for amendments to the 1965 act and drafted legislative proposals giving them control of both title and practice. These were ratified by NBASW in 1988 and passed through the provincial assembly as a private member's bill, coming into effect January 1989. Under this legislation people who are not members of NBASW commit an offence if they either practice social work or hold themselves out to be a social worker. Therefore, New Brunswick has achieved a level of occupational closure comparable to that in Newfoundland.

Prince Edward Island was the first Canadian province to enact mandatory registration for social workers. In 1985, the Prince Edward Island Association of Social Workers (PEIASW) applauded the minister's call for more professionally trained social workers. This encouragement was followed by legislative proposals:

> The PEI Association of Social Workers continues to focus much of
> its energy on drafting social work legislation that will provide for
> control of title and the registration of social workers. Discussions
> with government provide optimism that an act will be passed in the
> next sitting of the legislature. (*The Social Worker*, 1986, 54: 4, 186)

The association was told that legislation would be passed in 1987, and created a committee to negotiate with government. However, discussions broke down at the eleventh hour over compulsory registration. A compromise was presented to PEIASW members in January 1988.

> The present proposal includes (1) control of title, (2) voluntary
> registration, (3) control of Island designated social work positions
> in government (the employer of most social workers) and (4) a
> regulatory board. (*The Social Worker*, 1988, 56: 1, 39)

This would increase but not complete occupational closure. The legislation subsequently passed that year was "well received by members" as a "major step in establishing the professional profile of social work" in the province (*The Social Worker*, 1988, 56: 2, 86). Occupational closure in Prince Edward Island is not as complete as in Newfoundland and New Brunswick, for registration remains voluntary and control of practice is only secure in specified provincial government positions. Therefore, PEIASW has continued to argue for further professionalization of social work positions in provincial departments.

Quebec's Corporation Professionelle de Travailleurs Sociaux de Quebec (CPTSQ) was established in law in 1960. In the aftermath of Quebec's quiet revolution, which brought the Quebec professional class into existence and then to power, the social work profession (together with 37 other professional groups) was included in a new professional code brought into law in 1973 (Landry, 1990). This gave the CPTSQ control of the title "social worker," and of the initials R.S.W. and T.S.P. (Walsh, 1990). Thus professionalization in Quebec preceded that in other provinces, so CPTSQ has not shared the recent preoccupation with regulation that has dominated the agenda of Canada's other social work associations (Landry, 1990).

The Ontario Association of Professional Social Workers has the most resources of all Canada's provincial social work associations, even purchasing its own building in 1985. The 1800 members of the metropolitan Toronto branch were able to buy discount price blocks of seating at sports and entertainment events and to organize group travel plans and group insurance. Use of these perks to attract even more members was proposed. In spite of this strength, Ontario is the only province without legislation regulating the practice of social work (Gowanlock,

1986). The profession itself created the Ontario College of Certified Social Workers (OCCSW) in 1982 to confer "certification" on those with university degrees in social work, with two years of supervised experience, who have passed college exams and who agree to have their practice reviewed by peers. Certification is voluntary, and there are 2600 C.S.W.s in Ontario.

In 1985, the OAPSW initiated project legislation and published a report jointly with the college advocating increased regulation of social work practice. The director of the School of Social Work at York University chaired a steering committee to develop the argument for registration, to document social work's concerns about the provincial government's health professions legislative review and to gain support for either a government or a private bill to require registration of social workers. Project legislation faced a tough challenge for the provincial minister questioned the need for registration:

> The minister asked a number of questions that will require carefully considered awareness by the Association and College if the bid for legislation is to proceed further. He wanted to know what documented evidence exists that the public needs to be protected from unqualified people to call themselves social workers and the extent of this problem; who would be adversely affected by legislation that would give social workers exclusive practice rights; whether qualified social workers from other provinces would be automatically accepted in Ontario; where the community college trained social workers would fit into the legislation; and whether there are likely to be objections to the legislation from within the profession. (*The Social Worker*, 1986, 54: 3, 142)

The OAPSW and the OCCSW continued to lobby, sending reports to members, MPPs and employers, about the committee's efforts and politicians' responses on special project legislation letterhead. The association's proposals were discussed by a cabinet committee in July 1988 with presentation to full cabinet anticipated "soon."

While Ontario social workers were pursuing legislated registration, the provincial government was reviewing regulation for all health care professions. Twenty-four professions were considered including medicine, nursing, midwifery and chiropractic. Self-government was recommended for professions that might significantly harm patients, that were not closely supervised by another profession and that lacked "alternative" forms of regulation (Schwartz, 1989). The social work profession was excluded from the terms of reference of this study, and although the OAPSW and the OCCSW both made presentations, legislation for social workers was not considered in the final report. In the president's words:

> It is crucial for the social work profession that we exert pressure on
> the government to remind them that we mean business. We are a
> unified, determined profession taking responsible action to protect
> the public of Ontario. Social work legislation for Ontario is long
> overdue! (*The Social Worker,* 1989, 57: 3, 169)

In 1989, the Ministry of Community and Social Services released a discussion paper inviting response to key questions on social work regulation, using a format similar to that used for the health professions. Support for self-regulation of social work was not unanimous. Some bureaucrats outside the profession said self-regulation was not necessary because social workers were already supervised within the public service and in voluntary social services. Others were concerned about disenfranchising some service providers and saw social workers as placing undue attention on professional self-interest, fostering private practice and clinical emphases at the expense of macro practice (Turner, 1990). However, project legislation had caught the government's attention, which in June 1990 promised new social work legislation (OAPSW, nd.)

In September 1990, the Conservative government of Ontario was replaced by the New Democratic Party. Legislative initiatives were being considered by the new government, but after the resignation of one minister and the appointment of another, the NDP Premier announced in 1992 that "the regulation of social workers is not a priority for the government at this time" (OAPSW). The OAPSW continued to press for legislation and surveyed its membership to confirm that 77.1 per cent supported "the continuation of the pursuit of social work legislation as a priority goal of the association" and a continued levy from members to support this initiative (Hansen and Repko, 1993). The OAPSW has expressed frustration at its exclusion as a health care profession and its resultant distance from debates about the future of Ontario's health care system (Swail, 1992; MacKenzie Davis, 1993). The OAPSW is pursuing a private members.

The occupational closure strategies of social work associations in Ontario have been controversial. First, those opposing project legislation from within the profession have shared Alcock's (1990) view that those providing social work services in a variety of nontraditional settings are likely to be disadvantaged by occupational closure. For example, services to immigrants, to visible minorities and to indigenous Canadians are best provided by people from their respective backgrounds. Because of the economic and educational disadvantages associated with membership in a minority group, these workers have had difficulty accessing social work education. Similarly, their agencies are likely to have less funding than the mainstream agencies and less able to afford qualified social workers. In this context, occupational closure would first exclude such minority workers and then probably subordinate them as an underclass of workers operating under social work supervision. Those in self-help and feminist social services are also likely to be disadvantaged by occupational closure. For example, battered women, sexual abuse survivors, alcoholics in recovery and single parents in poverty can all be helpful to others with similar problems. With full occupational closure the activities of such workers, predominantly women, could be either excluded or subordinated.

The system of post secondary education in Ontario supports the occupational closure projects of social work. The community colleges provide two-year social work certificate programs whose graduates are excluded from registration under the OAPSW proposals. These are more accessible than university programs for minority, self-help and feminist workers in nontraditional agencies. However, there is no direct educational path from college programs into the university level B.S.W. programs, and to membership in the profession. Exceptions include Carleton University, which has an explicit commitment to affirmative action in admissions and to feminist and antiracist social work education, and Laurentian University, which includes a native human services program.

Manitoba has two social work associations — the Manitoba Association of Social Workers (MASW), and the Manitoba Institute of Registered Social Workers — through which, since 1966, social workers may obtain registration. Although there were 1200 social work positions in the province, and 75 per cent of incumbents were qualified as "professional" social workers, only 220 belonged to the MASW in 1988. The two associations first created a coalition and eventually unified in 1990 to increase the likelihood of achieving licensing (Masiowski, 1993). However, as of December 1993 the Manitoba social work profession had not achieved occupational closure (Cullen, 1994) but was waiting for the report of the Manitoba Law Reform Commission on professional regulation and was planning to respond to it.

Saskatchewan has had legislation since 1967 providing for voluntary registration of social workers and control of the title R.S.W. In 1985, the Saskatchewan Association of Social Workers (SASW) drafted legislative proposals for mandatory registration, protection of the title of "social worker" and a more "stringent" baseline for professional entry. After circulation to and feedback from government departments, unions, other professions and from social work educators, the SASW redrafted the proposals. Devine's Conservative government did not respond, but the NDP government elected in 1991 was more enthusiastic. New social work legislation received royal assent in May 1993, and resulted in a public appointment to the SASW council, stronger discipline provisions and protection of the title "social worker" (*Saskatchewan Social Worker*, 1993, 4: 2) but did not extend to control of practice. Anyone with a social work degree, or who has been in practice for five years, can be registered. Proclamation still had not been achieved by June 1994 because of disagreement over the status as social workers of human justice graduates at the University of Regina. This disagreement brought other concerns about elitism to the surface, and the NDP government abandoned the legislation.

Saskatchewan has a system of social work education explicitly encouraging access to the profession by disadvantaged groups. The University of Regina provides two-year certificate programs in social work, human justice and Indian social work, the latter through the Saskatchewan Indian Federated College, which can be combined with two years of arts and science courses to complete a professional degree in social work. Accessibility is increased by provisions allowing admission of adults who have not completed high school and by offering social work courses part time and in locations across the province. Hence, access to social work education in Saskatchewan is democratized so that successes in achieving occupational closure would be less damaging to vulnerable groups.

Alberta has had legislated voluntary registration and protection of the title R.S.W. since 1969. The Alberta Association of Social Workers (AASW) began the search for new legislation in 1986-87, and expected proclamation of the new social work professions act in the fall of 1993 (*The Advocate*, 1993, 18: 1). The association also worked on regulations and bylaws to implement the new legislation concerning speciality registries, rules of conduct, client access to files, recording frequency and assessment.

The profession in British Columbia is divided between the British Columbia Association of Social Workers (BCASW) and the Association of Professional Social Workers (APSW). In 1985, the BCASW wrote to all provincial members of the Legislative Assembly proposing compulsory registration and control of title for all social workers in private practice. The minister's rejection was published in *The Social Worker*. The number of full-time, registered social workers in British Columbia declined with government cutbacks, from 715 in 1982 to 538 in 1987. The profession also faced financial difficulties, with salaries falling behind those of nurses and psychologists and declining in their purchasing power since 1982. However, just before going to the people in 1991, the provincial government passed legislation requiring registration for all social workers in private practice. This private practice roster required "either an M.S.W. and four years of supervised experience" or other "exceptional circumstances" such as 12 years of practice and some formal social work education (*BCASW Perspectives*, 1991, 13:4). Social workers working with various public and private agencies, or engaged in social work education, did not have to be registered unless required by their employers. Some employers merely required evidence of eligibility for registration.

The social work profession in British Columbia has achieved the level of occupational closure required to protect the public from incompetent or unethical private practitioners. However, social workers in both the mainstream agencies and the nontraditional agencies serving minorities, survivors and other disadvantaged groups do not have to register. This solution suggests that in his home province, at least, Stuart Alcock's (1990) warnings about the elitist outcome of occupational closure may have been heeded.

Social work education in British Columbia has been divided between the University of British Columbia and the University of Victoria. The latter has developed within an explicit interprofessional faculty in which students from several professions study together. In addition, Victoria has the mandate to deliver social work education to rural British Columbia, including the province's native communities. The province's new university colleges in the interior have introduced several new social work education programs using the Victoria programs as a base.

Discussion and Conclusion

These recent strategies of occupational closure have had mixed results. Some have attained full occupational closure such as Newfoundland and New Brunswick; Ontario and Nova Scotia have achieved little change as yet. Social workers in British Columbia and Saskatchewan have taken limited steps toward occupational closure. These results are best evaluated by their impact on the most vulnerable and by their ability to combine quality of social service with democratized access to the ranks of the profession itself. If the profession is open to a cross section of the community in terms of class, ethnicity and cultural group, social work need not be a middle-class act exercised on the poor. Social work need not be gendered — work done by women to women but at the direction of men without understanding of the work. A number of implications emerge from this discussion.

First, occupational closure can result in subordination by or to another occupational group. This can happen to professional social workers when those who supervise them are not members of the same profession. When Newfoundland social workers attained occupational closure, they may have sacrificed their own autonomy to a class of male public sector managers who have been defined out of the profession of social work. It can also happen to paraprofessionals of various kinds when the substance of their work is controlled by social workers. The result is reduced autonomy for the subsidiary group. Deskilling results as professional tasks are overdefined in order to maintain control of the subsidiary group. Also, this process of subordination of paraprofessionals from minorities and other predominantly female groups, is inconsistent with social work commitments to equality and democracy.

Second, if we believe that this subordination of one class of social workers by another is unacceptable in terms of social work values, then various paraprofessional occupational groups must have access to social work education, and thereby ultimately, to full professional status. Issues related to academic access, which include upgrading, provisions for mature students, affirmative action, geographic access, cultural access and economic access, must be considered. Also, a continuum of social work education is needed that permits transfer of credit from the college social work certificate programs to the B.S.W. programs in the universities. The absence of a continuum is costly to both the student and to the state.

Third, occupational closure is practiced horizontally as well as vertically, as members of one profession attempt to exclude the members of another profession from work that is defined as within their own legitimate "scope of practice." Hence, nurses change dressings and social workers investigate child abuse. A pharmacist can put together a prescription but not prescribe. A chiropractor can not requisition an X-ray, and has to rely on a cooperative physician if he or she is to complete a thorough assessment. Thus, each profession has used horizontal occupational closure to identify areas in which it will have exclusive jurisdiction. However, complex health and social problems require services that may fall within the scope of practice of several aspiring occupations. Acute hospital care, community home care, extended care, mental health services, domestic violence intervention and various forms of rehabilitation all involve multiple professions. Most of the practitioners providing these services have been involved in separatist professional education, which has incorporated an historic definition of scope of practice into a professional ideology. This ideology supports continued strategies of occupational closure, both at the level of the professional organization and at the level of the specific institution or program (Gross and Gross, 1987), thereby reducing effectiveness and efficiency. Students in professional schools can be brought together in the classroom to study the institutions and programs in which they jointly serve and the closure strategies of other occupational groups (Bella, 1990). Professional schools can be brought together under a single faculty, as at the University of Victoria for example, to facilitate the timetable and curricular coordination required for such an initiative. This would prepare students for collaboration in the field, and could make interprofessional competition less destructive.

Fourth and finally, the call for increased professionalization must be continually questioned and analyzed rather than accepted as a self-evident truth. Stuart Alcock's (1990) original question, "Whose interests are served by social work registration?", needs to be asked again and again. The support for social work registration is phrased in terms of claims to serve the public interest. However, the truth of these claims must be evaluated on its own merit. Some claim, for example, that the increased professional power resulting from compulsory registration will permit social workers to resist bureaucratic instructions that require they do something contrary to the Social Work Code of Ethics (Kimberly and Rowe, 1990a; 1990b). However, a court case in Newfoundland in 1985 showed that professional ethics were overridden by the obligation to serve one's employer (Lundy and Gauthier, 1989). We do not know if the courts would interpret this any differently following passage of the province's recent social work legislation. Others claim that increased power will accrue to professional organizations themselves, and that this will be used to serve the public interest. However, the recent occupational closure strategies of Canada's anglophone social work associations have necessitated cooperation with government. Confrontations with government have probably been avoided in order to retain government support for social work legislation. If this conservatism continues after successful occupational closure, then the increased power resulting from occupational closure will not have been used in the public interest. Others claim that the credentialling and discipline provisions involved in implementing registration and control of title will ensure quality of service. However, this will only be true if discipline provisions are well publicized and accessible. Recently revealed experiences of those who have been sexually abused by their physicians suggest that complaint systems are not necessarily accessible or user friendly (Whitman, 1993).

The professionalization of social work poses a dilemma for women. It offers opportunities for increased status at the same time it has the potential to introduce conflict and competition both within the profession itself and across professions.

Endnotes

[1]   News item in *The Social Worker* and in the newsletters of the provincial associations published on or before December 31, 1993 were researched for this chapter, with added correspondence, phone calls and facsimiles providing clarification where needed. Thanks are due to CASW (for access to their collection of provincial newsletters), and to provincial associations who responded to my inquiries. Any errors, omissions or interpretations are my own responsibility.

References

Alcock, S. 1990. "Licensing the Social Work Profession, Who For?" *The Social Worker*. 58: 1, 27-28.

Baines, C. T. 1991. "The Professions and an Ethic of Care" in Baines, Carol T., Patricia Evans and Sheila Neysmith (eds.), *Women's Caring: Feminist Perspectives on Social Welfare*. Toronto: McClelland and Stewart.

Bella, L. 1989. "The Canadian Social Work Profession 1985-1989: Professional Self-Interest and Public Welfare." CASSW, Laval, Quebec.

Bella, L. 1990. "Competitive Professionalism: Implications for Social Work Education." CASSW, Victoria.

Bella, L. 1991. "Doctors, Social Workers and Nurses: Hyphenated Liberals" in Kirwin, Bill (ed.), *Ideology, Development and Social Welfare*, 2nd edition. Toronto: Canadian Scholars' Press, pp. 163-186.

Bella, L. 1992. "Feminist Scholarship in a Professional School." *Oval Works: Feminist Social Work Scholarship*. St. John's: School of Social Work, Memorial University. pp. 41-60.

Campbell, M. 1988. "Management as 'Ruling': A Class Phenomenon in Nursing." *Studies in Political Economy*. 27: 29-49.

Coburn, D., Torrance, G. M. and Kaufer, J. M. 1983. "Medical Dominance in Canada in Historical Perspective: The Rise and Fall of Medicine." *International Journal of Health Services*. 13: 3, 407-432.

Coburn, D. and Biggs. C. L. 1986. "Limits to Medical Dominance: The Case of Chiropractic." *Social Science and Medicine*. 22: 10, 1035-1046.

Cullen, D. 1994. January 11th personal communication to Leslie Bella.

Ehrenreich, B. and English, D.. 1973. *Witches, Midwives and Nurses: The History of Women Healers*. : The Feminist Press.

Etzioni, A. 1969. *The Semi-Professions and Their Organization*. New York: Free Press.

Friedson, E. 1970. *The Profession of Medicine*. New York: Harper and Row.

Gowanlock, G. 1986. *Social Work Regulation in Canada: 1926-1982*. Ottawa: CASW.

Gowanlock, G. 1990. "Social Work Regulation in Canada: One Historical Perspective." *The Social Worker*. 58: 1, 6-8.

Gross, A. M. and Gross, J. 1987. "Attitudes of Physicians and Nurses Towards the Role of Social Workers in Primary Health Care: What Promotes Collaboration?" *Family Practice*. 4: 4, 266-270.

Hamowy, R. 1984. *Canadian Medicine: A Study in Restricted Entry*. Vancouver: Fraser Institute.

Hansen, F. (Bud) and Repko, K. 1993. "Support for the Pursuit of Social Work Registration: An Executive Summary" *OAPSW Newsmagazine*. 20: 1, 24.

Hurl, L. 1983. *Building a Profession: The Origin and Development of the Department of Social Service in the University of Toronto 1914-1918*. Toronto: Faculty of Social Work, University of Toronto.

Johnson, T. J. 1972. *Professions and Power*. London: Macmillan.

Keddy B. et al. 1986. "The Doctor Nurse Relationship: An Historical Perspective." *Journal of Advanced Nursing*. 11: 745-753.

Kimberly, D. and Rowe, W. 1991a. "Mount Cashel: What Went Wrong? Part I: Issues for the Profession." *The Social Worker.* 59: 2, 85-90.

Kimberly, D. and Rowe, W. 1991a. "Mount Cashel: What Went Wrong? Part II: Issues in the Administration of Child Protection." *The Social Worker.* 59: 3, 133-137.

Landry, P. 1990. "Reconnaissance Professionelle: Le Case de Travailleurs Sociaux du Quebec." *The Social Worker.* 58: 1, 9-13.

Larson, M. S. 1977. *The Rise of Professionalism: A Sociological Analysis.* Berkely: University of California Press.

Lundy, C. and Gauthier, L. 1989. "Social Work Practice and the Master-Servant Relationship." *The Social Worker,* 57: 4, 190-193.

MacKenzie Davis, J. 1993. "Strategic Directions for Social Work and OAPSW in the 1990's." *OAPSW Newsmagazine.* 20: 2, 4-6.

Masiowski, E. 1993. "From the President's Pen." *Manitoba Social Worker.* 26: 1, 3.

Maton, B. 1988. "Social Work Regulation in the Canadian Provinces: Prospects and Problems." *Canadian Social Work Review.* 5: 1, 78-90.

Melosh, B. 1989. "'Not Merely a Profession': Nurses and Resistance to Professionalization." *American Behavioural Scientist.* 32: 6, 668-679.

OAPSW. n.d. "Social Work Legislation: (i) History, (ii) Questions and Answers, (iii) Key Points" and "Fact Sheet on Need for Social Work Regulation in Ontario."

Parkin, F. 1979. *Marxism and Class Theory: A Bourgeois Critique.* London: Tavistock.

Richmond, M. 1917. *Social Diagnosis.* New York: Russell Sage.

Schwartz, A. M. 1989. *Striking a New Balance: A Blue Print for Regulation of Ontario's Health Professions.* Ontario: Health Professions Review.

Struthers, J. 1987. "'Lord Give us Men': Women and Social Work in English Canada, 1918 to 1953," in Moscovitch, Allan and Jim Albert (eds.), *The "Benevolent" State: The Growth of Welfare in Canada.* Toronto: Garamond, pp. 111-125.

Swail, A. 1992. "RHPA Update: Repercussions of the Regulated Health Professions Act as Passed in 1991." *OAPSW Metronews.* (March) 16-17.

Turner, F. 1990. "Preliminary Comments." *The Social Worker.* 58: 1, 4.

Walsh, M. 1990a. "Regulation of Social Work Practice in Canada: Issues, Achievements, Costs and Challenges." *The Social Worker.* 58: 1, 14-16.

Walsh, M. 1990b. "Status of Social Work Legislation Across Canada." *The Social Worker.* 58: 1, 17-19.

Warrington-Turcke, K. 1983. "Evolution of Accountability in Nursing in Canada." *The Canadian Nurse.* 79: 1, 34-37.

Whitman, L. 1993. *No Ordinary Trust: The Patient Doctor Relationship: The Final Report of the Committee to Investigate the Process of Reporting Sexual Misconduct by Physicians Towards Patients.* St. John's: Newfoundland Medical Board.

Wilding, P. 1982. *Professional Power and Social Welfare.* London: Routledge.

Witz, A. 1992. *Professions and Patriarchy.* London: Routledge.

Chapter VIII
Student Reflections on the Future of Social Work Education

Katherine Lanigan Chan
Kathleen Connors Dilworth

This chapter explores a few of the ways in which alternative paradigms, such as feminist and transpersonal theory, might alleviate some of the deficiencies in current social work education. The incorporation of other paradigms into current social work curriculum may also provide the profession with a revitalized vision and direction for the next century.

Women and the social work profession have always been associated with one another. Historically, women and social workers have been considered society's natural caregivers.

> Caring refers to the mental, emotional and physical effort involved in looking after, responding to and supporting others. In our society, most of this work is done by women in varying forms throughout their lives. It is done as mothers, daughters and wives in the context of individual relationships, in the community as volunteers, through the professions of nursing, social work and teaching. (Baines, Evans and Neysmith, 1991, p. 11).

At its inception, social work required no special qualities save a kindred heart and a willing hand. This tradition has allowed contemporary social work practice — a profession requiring a level of ability and skill earned through years of training and experience — to continue to be devalued by a patriarchal society.

The profession of social work emerged from charity work in the latter half of the nineteenth century. Although it has evolved from a preprofessional into a professional stage (Baines, Evans, and Neysmith, 1992), it has yet to be fully recognized as a profession such as nursing, psychology and teaching. One reason perhaps is a dual focus on individual and social change (Morell, 1987). Social work has struggled to integrate these two facets of practice as a means to distinguish itself from other professions. However, its attempts to reconcile these two perspectives have contributed to the profession's difficulty articulating social work's unique knowledge, values and skills. Another reason for the perception of social work as a "soft" or semi profession is that the foundation of practice is caring. This caring aspect is the source of direct practice and also the force behind legislative and administrative policy changes and social movements. But, as Baines et al. state: "Caring is frequently invisible, usually devalued and generally assigned to women" (Baines et al., 1992, p. 25). Because the caring work that women do is so undervalued in our culture, it is also devalued as a component of the social work profession:

> the task of social workers is to integrate an ethic of care into professional practice in a way that does not reify caring as women's "natural" work.... As a first step, caring must be viewed as a source of both women's oppression and women's strengths.... A feminist perspective in social work reframes many of the deficits attributed to women clients as strengths. It begins by reclaiming the history of women in social work, valuing what women have done in the profession, enhancing women's sense of control, accepting diversity, and developing a theoretical base from the experiences of women. (Baines et al., 1992, p. 27)

Today, the profession of social work remains a predominantly female profession. The majority of those involved in education, practice and utilization are women. Yet social work education, for the most part, demands that female students change themselves to fit a male-dominant conception of the profession, recreating within its ranks the very patriarchal system social work professes to challenge. Women in the social work profession are concentrated in direct practice areas and move in a lateral direction, whereas males ascend to administrative roles either in practice or educational settings (Williams, 1992).

By applying alternative paradigms such as feminist and transpersonal theory to social work education, educators can address some of the deficiencies in the current social work curriculum and move the profession into the future. To ensure that the social work profession begins to meet the needs of future practitioners and clients — the majority of whom will be female — social work education must change. It must take the profession in a new and more viable direction, one which builds upon the strengths of the female practitioner and client. In this way, the caring and helping characteristics of the social work profession may be transformed from something considered to be an innate female characteristic into an economic and political force. Social work education requires an innovative approach in order to broaden its current knowledge base and move into the next century. Alternative paradigms, such as feminist and transpersonal theory, may provide the vision necessary to accomplish these goals.

Feminist Theory and Social Work Education

Social work and nineteenth-century feminism share a common value base, stressing the importance of "human rights,, social justice and gender equality" (Ramsay, 1991, p. 33). However, because the empirical method dominated thinking, the knowledge base and values of both social work and feminism have been largely ignored. Both perspectives share a belief in the "release of human power and of social power" (Morell, 1987, p. 153) in an ethic of caring, which is a central focus in social work practice, and in the creation of a just society.

In spite of frequent debate pertaining to the nature of feminist contribution to social work education, a case can be made for adopting feminist thought and principles in some form.

> Clearly a phenomenon of significance has emerged, be it a thought system, a value orientation, a set of skills or some constellation of these. Whether we call it feminist counselling, feminist therapy or feminist social work practice, this evolving way of helping, offered primarily by women to women, should be understood in the context of contemporary feminism. (Valentich, 1986, p. 565)

As feminism is incorporated into the social work knowledge base, it can increase the profession's responsiveness to the needs of women.

Feminist theory and social work share the dual focus of individual and social concerns (Morell, 1987). Feminist theory seeks to emphasize and validate women's experience and ways of learning. Knowledge traditionally associated with males — that which is measurable, quantifiable, hierarchical — remains the yardstick against which women's ways of learning and organizing knowledge are held and found wanting. Dore discusses Wetzel's three main principles of feminism: "(1) the unity of all living things, events and knowledge; (2) the uniqueness of the individual; and (3) personal power and responsibility" (Dore, 1994, p. 97). These principles are compatible with social work knowledge and values. The application of these principles to the social work classroom, where 80 per cent of the students are women, is the only one that recognizes the unique challenges women face in the current educational system.

The distinctive needs of women students are clearly addressed by feminist pedagogy, which "applies feminist principles and values to the methodology of teaching" (Dore, 1994, p. 98). Dore discusses the three barriers to adult learning that particularly apply to women — the intuitive/affective barrier, the ethical barrier and the critical/logical barrier. The first, the intuitive/affective barrier, prevents women from learning because their lifetime socialization creates in them a feeling of personal inadequacy in the classroom. The second, the ethical barrier, arises when a student's fundamental principles are challenged in the educational setting. Finally, the critical/logical barrier is created "when new learning does not fit into the existing thought structure, [it] results in cognitive dissonance for the student" (Dore, 1994, p. 99). Traditional learning situations do little to meet the particular needs of adult women students. Dore summarizes the goals of feminist pedagogy as

> (1) empowerment of all participants in the learning process, students as well as teacher; (2) development of a sense of community in which all share equally in the learning task; and (3) the realization of the capacity for leadership as an outgrowth of taking responsibility for one's own learning and the learning of others. (Dore, 1994, p. 100)

This style of teaching addresses the needs of adult women students. These goals provide a way to prepare future practitioners to meet the needs of women clients and society more effectively. Collins argues for the incorporation of feminist theory into the social work knowledge base:

> The social work profession needs to understand and incorporate feminist perspectives and theories — not solely as these pertain to the personal lives and problems of females as clients or as social workers — but as paradigmatic ways of understanding our patriarchal culture, its masculine ethos, and the inevitable conflict between it and what social workers and feminists want for humanity and society. (Collins, 1986, p. 214)

This alternative perspective provides a process and a product consistent with social work's vision for the future.

Transpersonal Theory and Social Work

Transpersonal psychology offers a comprehensive perspective that can inform and transform social work curriculum and practice (Cowley and Derezotes, 1994).

Transpersonal theory provides a basis for social work to develop a holistic paradigm shift. This paradigm could also transform the perception of social work and create a climate of mutual respect and collaboration with other helping professions. Richard Ramsay (1991) and Ann Weick (1987) summarize the history of Western thought to provide a framework for understanding the development of contemporary world views. Modern scientific theory arose from the reductionist, empirical science of Galileo, Kepler and Newton. This model resulted in increased understanding of physical nature and led to major breakthroughs in medical science. At one time this approach was thought to be the only one worthy of merit, and empirical knowledge was regarded as the only kind of knowledge — a phenomenon that could not be measured was dismissed as nonscientific. This Cartesian-Newtonian model reigned supreme for centuries and was imposed upon social work practice by the Flexner report of 1915 (Austin, 1983). Flexner's definition of a profession underrated practice wisdom because it lacked a systematic, empirical basis. Social work accepted this report's negative perception of the profession as valid criticism (Austin, 1983).

Even science, however, no longer fully adheres to its old models of reality. Quantum physics, relativity theory and chaos theory are part of a scientific revolution that promotes a new paradigm. Holistic, ecological approaches developed from this paradigm. Ramsay notes that "instead of a mechanical 'building block' view of the world . . . nature functions more like a web of ' dancing' relationships between the component parts of a unified whole" (Ramsay, 1991, p. 36). It is a world of chaos, not equilibrium, where change is the only constant. This paradigm is a shift from linear to nonlinear thinking, and thus multiple possibilities for change exist. Scientific thought precedes the world view, which remains strongly rooted in the empirical, mechanistic model. This may begin to account for the resistance to the incorporation of alternative paradigms such as feminist and transpersonal theory, which is often apparent in some curriculums.

Transpersonal psychology supports the foundations of social work and feminist theory. Transpersonal theory is a synthesis of Eastern contemplative practice and Western psychology, which integrates philosophy with modern science. The underlying vision of transpersonal theory expands human potential beyond the ego, beyond Maslow's notion of self-actualization, into higher states of consciousness (Cowley and Derezotes, 1994). Like social work theory, it has a dual, psychosocial focus that includes "physical, emotional, cognitive, cultural, organizational or sociopolitical" (Cowley and Derezotes, 1994, p. 33). The goals of transpersonal psychology are self-transcendence on the personal level and a sense of global communion. Like early social work, transpersonal theory acknowledges the spiritual dimension. In modern social work practice this perspective is often ignored. In an effort to be politically correct and respect diversity in modern society, we often address religious differences by denying the spiritual aspect of human experience. In doing so, we leave out a critical component in a holistic approach. In transpersonal psychology, this spiritual dimension is seen as the life force within each individual, which transcends individual beings and unites all living things (Cowley and Derezotes, 1994).

Wilbur (1979) speaks of development and consciousness as an evolutionary process that is never instantaneous. He describes five levels of consciousness: the persona level, the ego level, the total organism level, the transpersonal bands and unity consciousness. He presents therapies for each level of consciousness. Although Wilbur's language is rooted in hierarchies and linear thought, his intent is to examine the spectrum of human consciousness and offer an alternative to pathologically oriented models of thought. In psychological terms,

> the self...eventually dis-identifies with its present structure so as to identify with the next higher-order emergent structure. It doesn't throw the basic structure away, it simply no longer exclusively identifies with it.... Every time a higher-order deep structure emerges, the lower-order structures are subsumed, enveloped or comprehended by it. (Wilbur, 1990, pp. 102-103)

This essentially means that we don't completely let go of a long-held world view. Once we have comprehended a new vision of the world, we cease to identify with the previous one. An alternative theory such as transpersonal psychology "offers hope because it may well be the only paradigm sufficiently integrative and 'big' enough to deal with the complex, multidimensional and interrelated personal, familial, societal and global issues that beg for amelioration in the 1990s" (Cowley and Derezotes, 1994, p. 36).

This perception is congruent with holistic social work practice, emphasizing the dynamic, complex interaction between the person and the total environment. In the past, social caseworkers tended to focus on problems and deficiencies in clients and saw themselves as psychosocial "gurus" with the correct treatment solutions (Specht, 1990). But at the same time social work theory has espoused the values and ideas currently present in the new paradigm. Perlman notes that recent behavioural science research supports "the conviction on which some few of us had long operated: that insofar as feasible the client himself must be helped to be *active in coping*, active beyond 'telling'" (Perlman, 1989, p. 224). Weick discusses the problem focus of social work and argues the merits of a strengths perspective. She quotes Ruth Smalley's view that the

...underlying purpose of all social work effort is to release human power in individuals for personal fulfilment and social good, and to release social power for the creation of the kinds of society, social institutions, and social policy which make self-realization possible for all. (Weick, 1989, p. 352)

The new paradigm is based, not on authority and competition, but on equality and cooperation. It recognizes interdependence and the need to focus professional attention upon issues facing the postmodern world.

Social Work Education: Problems and Possibilities

Higher education is expected to challenge students to question and explore. In reality, however, it is a hierarchical structure where the "expert" imparts knowledge to the student, whose role is simply to receive this knowledge. The price paid for this one-directional transfer is the suppression of all inquiry, creativity and mutuality. In addition, the knowledge base of the present academic curriculum, which is considered expansive, is actually embedded within the dominant, patriarchal culture. It is not objective, neutral nor open to critique. Florence Howe observes:

> In the broadest context of that word, teaching is a political act: some person is choosing, for whatever reasons, to teach a set of values, ideas, assumptions and pieces of information, and in so doing, to omit other values, ideas, assumptions and pieces of information. If all those choices form a pattern excluding half the human race, that is a political act one can hardly help noticing. To omit women entirely makes one kind of political statement; to include women as a target for humour makes another. To include women with seriousness and vision, and with some attention to the perspective of women as a hitherto subordinate group is simply another kind of political act. Education is the kind of political act that controls destinies, gives some persons hope for a particular kind of future and deprives others even of ordinary expectations for work and achievement. (Howe, 1984)

There are several deficits in the current social work curriculum. Undergraduate social work education generally prepares students to accept the status quo and to focus on helping clients adjust themselves to their environment. Gender issues, ethnic, cultural and religious diversity are inadequately addressed, while the spiritual and transpersonal dimensions are rarely even acknowledged. Student education in macro practice is often limited to a single semester course, which would seem to be insufficient in today's society. In the case of elective courses, the students who register in these are most be those already sensitive to ethnic, racial, cultural and religious diversity and to the oppression of women in our society. The mainstream curriculum, while seeming to provide an adequate foundation in traditional social work knowledge, values and skills, may only offer an inadequate foundation for future social work practice. Future students may enter the profession with insufficient knowledge and vision to work effectively with tomorrow's individuals and client groups. The underlying problem is that we fail to recognize that we are perceiving the universe and operating within it from a narrow set of values, ideas and assumptions endemic to social work education.

In the past, social work educators have attempted to solve the profession's gender identity crisis by tacking material on women's issues onto existing curriculum. They have dealt with multicultural issues in the same manner. However, this method cannot accomplish the change in knowledge base and skills which may be necessary for the future. It "does not, in itself, guarantee the elimination of the inequities based on false generalizations that permeate the intellectual frameworks of social work knowledge" (Tice, 1990, p. 134).

The struggle to establish social work as a profession has resulted in a kind of isolationism. Social work curriculum may be unconsciously screening out knowledge from other sources, or transforming alternative theories into acceptable, social work language which may fail to clearly articulate the scope and depth of human experience. This is done by precluding interdisciplinary approaches that have the potential to broaden the scope of students' knowledge base and practice wisdom. If we look at the evolution of scientific thought, at human history, the very notion of discrete fields of study becomes an absurdity. The past efforts of social work to gain professional recognition have been conditioned by the old, reductionist model, which can never provide legitimacy to social work. Alternative perspectives, such as feminist theory and transpersonal theory, may develop and deepen the theoretical underpinnings of the profession.

The Process of Curriculum Change

Although many involved in social work education agree that curriculum must evolve to meet the future needs of the profession, change is often difficult. In order to more fully comprehend continuing resistance to curriculum transformation, it may be helpful to understand the process that would probably be involved in its reform.

Andersen (1987) and Tice (1990) described the theories developed by several scholars that might direct the on-going process of curriculum reformulation. Tice described social work curriculum change as existing at three different levels — compensatory, transformative and experienced curriculum. The first, "compensatory stage" of social work curriculum simply decrees that content addressing the issues of women and minorities must be added to traditional curriculum (Tice, 1990, p. 137). This is the "add a woman and stir" approach (Andersen, 1987) generally used to update course content by many faculties during the past two decades.

In the second, the "transformation stage," the knowledge base of social work education is minimally reformulated. The validity of traditional paradigms is questioned and previously hidden issues, such as social work's failure to appreciate the special needs of women, are considered. In this stage, this is the most important question social work educators need to ask: "What is the core content of [social work] and how would it have to change to reflect the fact that women are a majority of the world's population, whites are a minority of that population and race, sex and class stratification have structured social life?" (Tice, 1990, p. 138).

The third stage, the "experienced curriculum," as delineated by Tice gives the social work profession direction for the future. An experienced curriculum is a course of study that utilizes methods of instruction and field practice that "do not replicate racism, sexism and classism" (Tice, 1990, p. 138). Furthermore, "to achieve this goal, social work educators need to provide opportunities for students to understand and critique themselves, their relationships, and their histories. Self-esteem and independence must be enhanced if students are to become agents of change and recognize that the status quo is neither fixed nor natural" (Tice, 1990, p. 138).

The Problem of Resistance

Many members of the social work profession concede that education needs to take a new direction; there remains, however, a resistance to the adoption of a curriculum that would meet the future requirements of the social work profession. This problem pervades all levels of social work education — administration, faculty, field instruction and the student body.

The barriers and resistance to curriculum reformulation are formidable. "Institutions of higher education present potent barriers to the implementation of curricular reform to the extent that they perpetuate paradigms of the dominant culture. Academic councils and course approval processes exert their role as powerful shapers of academic discourse" (Tice, 1990, p. 140). Changes in curriculum, however desirable, are difficult to implement at the university level.

In their article, "Trying Transformations," Aiken et al. (1987) discuss the resistance they experienced as instructors of a semester-long, interdisciplinary seminar for faculty on feminist curriculum integration. While "many participants made measurable alterations in the perspective and content of their courses, alterations that will perhaps be extended and elaborated in years to come" (Aiken et al., p. 258), they eventually realized that they had "seriously underestimated the magnitude and intractability of the resistances they would confront. These proved hydra-like; no sooner had they sought to deal with one than another would arise" (Aiken et al., p. 258). Faculty resistance to feminist curriculum integration took many forms during the implementation of their project — from complete negation to an agreement to "shoehorn" a minimal amount of materials on women into their courses at a future date (Aiken et al., 1987, pp. 259-260). In fact, Tice believes that, as social work education vies for legitimate recognition within the arena of higher education, the profession's "historical embrace of empiricism and its paradigmatic norms of neutrality, objectivity and rationality may, in part, account for the lukewarm reception of feminist scholarship by the profession" (Tice, 1990, p. 140). In addition to faculty, fieldwork also presents obstacles and resistance to the incorporation of innovative world views into the social work curriculum.

The experience of field practice is paramount to a complete social work education. Yet, fieldwork may be less than satisfactory in supporting the knowledge base classroom learning provides.

> Application of information about gender bias in social work beyond the classroom is needed because of the centrality of field experience to social work education. Barriers (to the natural evolution of nonsexist field experiences) include those endemic to the systems and individuals involved in the field program. Given the nature of the systems involved and the unlikelihood of evolutionary change, changes should be initiated by social work faculty. (Berkun, 1984, p. 5)

However, this is rarely accomplished. Richard discusses the resistance many social work students face when they espouse any alternatives to traditional paradigms, such as feminism, during their field placements. Richard believes that most Canadian social work agencies and field instructors "obscure reality by denying social changes that are feminist inspired" (Richard, 1990, p. 8). Further, she asserts that a social work student's feminism is often overtly opposed in many agencies and by many field instructors through the constant questioning of the validity, scope and effectiveness of feminist theory. Students are often forced to hide their fundamental feminist beliefs to finish their placement requirements successfully.

Students often present their own resistances to feminist curriculum transformation. Vinton and Nelson-Gardell found that students often reject any inference that they are studying within a patriarchal educational system. "Female students who came of age during the 1980s tend to resist the notion that they or women in general are oppressed, and male students also see oppression as a thing of the past" (Vinton and Nelson-Gardell, 1993, p. 91).

Teaching strategies based on feminist pedagogy could assist "instructors" to implement the author's recommendation that to overcome this resistance "educators must meet students where they are. In other words, information should be delivered using formats that are congruent with the developmental stage of most of the students" (Vinton and Nelson-Gardell, 1993, p. 100). Kirst-Ashman also discusses the barriers and resistances students create when confronted with curriculum reformulation. "Students frequently resist the concept of feminism, challenge its validity and cling doggedly to the traditional acceptance of the sexist world they know" (Kirst-Ashman, 1992, p. 13). In fact, Kirst-Ashman believes that the process of accepting feminist ideals is so difficult for some students that she likens it to the stages a dying person goes through, as described by famed author Elizabeth Kubler-Ross. However, there are indicators that past resistance to the inclusion of alternative paradigms in social work curriculum and practice is weakening.

Some social work educators have attempted to include and evaluate the impact of such alternative ideologies on the attitudes and abilities of their students. For example, a group of Canadian researchers studied the effects of feminist social work education on several classes of undergraduate students (Pennell, et al., 1993). Although the authors of this study concluded that "their research is at an exploratory level and [they] present their ideas as hypotheses rather than as definitive conclusions" (Pennell, et al., p. 335), they state that "in all classes, the students ' feminist identification increased, practice approaches changed, and self-esteem was enhanced" (Pennell et al., p. 317). The student subjects themselves noted that "feminist social work education made a significant and worthwhile contribution to their professional and personal development" (Pennell, et al., p. 334). Approaches other than feminist theory have also been explored as legitimate additions to the social work knowledge base.

In his evaluation of several alternative approaches to social work practice, *Personal Deficiency, Ecological and Political Economy,* Canadian author John Coates states his belief that, despite the social work practitioner's personal theoretical preference, "the assumptions inherent in each approach result in different problem definitions and practice interventions" (Coates, 1992, p. 15). Therefore, it is not surprising that there has always been a certain level of resistance to social work curriculum transformation. However, Coates concludes that:

> if students are to maintain and carry forward a commitment to social change they must have taken as their own, that is internalized a new perspective, and not merely conformed to what they think others expect. To accomplish this goal educators must provide a structure that supports and facilitates personal and political transformation. (Coates, 1992, p. 29).

If the profession is to meet the needs of society in the future, these issues are worth further exploration and study by social work educators and practitioners.

Future Implications for Practitioners, Students and Educators

Social work practitioners, both administrative and frontline workers, have good reason to re-evaluate their role as clinicians, administrators, colleagues, field instructors and policy makers. They may need to challenge the status quo to serve their clients in a more holistic manner. They may also need to reawaken in themselves a sense of vocation that has all but disappeared in the modern world.

This can happen simultaneously on several levels. In work with individuals, social workers can connect with, empower and help clients to recognize in themselves and in their environment the conditions that impinge upon their growth. In working with groups, practitioners can help them to organize and develop leadership skills necessary to work collectively for social change. On a larger scale, social workers can also become adept at using the political forum as a means of bringing about positive social change.

Students can take more responsibility for their own educational and field experiences. They can develop strategies to exert pressure on the educational system to expand its vision beyond the authoritarian model. They can continue to question the assumptions of mainstream culture.

> We, within the institution, would not survive, we would not continue, if there wasn't political pressure from outside. If there weren't the interest expressed by these feminist students then, and the university didn't realize that these were the ones who were filling these huge classes and bringing in their tuition fees, then the powers that be, who don't want it to happen, wouldn't let it happen. (Eichler, 1992, p. 130)

This speaks to the tremendous power students have in shaping the future of education. Students can create a need for curriculum transformation by demanding courses that are sensitive to present reality and insisting on a curriculum that will adequately prepare them for practice in the postmodern world.

Social work educators face a challenge and a responsibility for the future direction of social work education and practice. Change can take place in many areas, but it is the educational context that will give shape to the social work profession of the future. Social work educators can play a unique role in leading the profession into the next century.

Faculty facing the difficult task of curriculum transformation require an atmosphere that supports and fosters this endeavour. Tice (1990) offers several suggestions that include in-service training, provision of curriculum materials and interdisciplinary seminars for faculty. To be effectively implemented in schools of social work, these changes require a context of mutual respect, support and collaboration.

The potential exists for social work education to play a central role in general curriculum transformation. If the role of clinicians is to release and reinforce the strengths within clients and social systems, then the role of social work educators is to release and reinforce strength in social work students. To do this, faculty and students must create conducive classroom conditions. For example, rather than simply presenting Biestek's casework principles, educators can model these principles to students. This would foster in students a greater sense of competence, strength and creative vision. Alternative paradigms, such as a transpersonal theory, may provide the basis for this innovative view of the profession.

> In the 1990s, social work educators have an opportunity to provide leadership, as professional and lay helpers seek to attend to the ills of the spiritual dimension. By integrating...transpersonal theory into its current perspective, social work education could "reconnect" with the profession's spiritual and religious origins in philanthropy, theology and moralism. As Weick (1992) so aptly observed, "When artistic practice joins with value commitment, social work can indeed be a force in society." (Cowley and Derezotes, 1994, p. 39)

There is a clear need for a transformation that supports the fundamental dignity of all people and the creation of a just society. Social work shares with feminism and transpersonal theory a vision of human experience that is dynamic, expansive and creative. As paradigms are allowed to interact, moreover, they may influence each other. For example the transpersonal paradigm has the potential to radically alter or give new dimensions to the feminist perspective. Other alternative world views, if explored and incorporated, also have the potential to broaden and transform the profession's theory base. Social work principles support a belief in the inner wisdom and potential for growth and development that we all possess. While the profession has espoused these values in theory, it has not always based practice or curriculum on this foundation.

The feminist conviction that "the personal is political" (Morell, 1987, p. 148) can be integrated into our practice. Feminism can be deepened by the transpersonal belief that "personal is spiritual." Professional social work organizations could take a leading role in promoting a sense of social justice and in developing in social workers a sense of the relationship between the personal (in its spiritual dimensions) and political. As Morell states, "feminist practitioners politicize individual services and personalize social structures" (Morell, 1987, p. 149). In this way, the dual nature of social work becomes a unified endeavour. When this happens, social work "promises to provide the energy, the analysis and the power required to transform our preference for social justice into a practice of social justice. The release of human power and of social power may then become not merely our goal but our activity" (Morell, 1987, p. 153). As different disciplines explore the possibilities of a more holistic paradigm, the foundations of social work theory and practice can only be strengthened. Social work can influence this shift in world views and become an equal partner in the development of more comprehensive helping interventions.

References

Aiken, S. H., Anderson, K., Dinnerstein, M., Lensink, J. and MacCorquodale, P. 1987. "Trying Transformations: Curriculum Integration and the Problem of Resistance." *Signs: Journal of Women in Culture and Society.* 12: 2, 255-275.

Andersen, M. L. 1987. "Changing the Curriculum in Higher Education." *Signs: Journal of Women in Culture and Society.* 12: 2, 222-240.

Austin, D. M. 1983. "The Flexner Myth and the History of Social Work." *Social Service Review.* (September) 357-377.

Baines, C. T., Evans, P. M. and Neysmith, S. M. (eds.). 1991. *Women's Caring: Feminist Perspectives on Social Welfare.* Toronto: McClelland and Stewart.

Baines, C. T., Evans, P. M. and Neysmith, S. M. 1992. "Confronting Women's Caring: Challenges for Practice and Policy." *AFFILIA.* 7: 1, 21-44.

Berkun, C. S. 1984. "Women and the Field Experience: Toward a Model of Nonsexist Field-Based Learning Conditions." *Journal of Education for Social Work.* 20: 3, 5-12.

Coates, J. 1992. "Ideology and Education for Social Work Practice." *Journal of Progressive Human Services* 3(2):15-30.

Collins, B. G. 1986. "Defining Feminist Social Work." *Social Work.* 31: 3, 214-219.

Cowley, A. S. and Derezotes, D. 1994. "Transpersonal Psychology and Social Work Education." *Journal of Social Work Education.* 30: 1, 32-41.

Dore, M. M. 1994. "Feminist Pedagogy and the Teaching of Social Work Practice." *Journal of Social Work Education.* (Winter) 30: 1, 97-106.

Eichler, M. 1992. "Not Always an Easy Alliance: The Relationship between Women's Studies and the Women's Movement in Canada," in Backhouse, C. and D. H. Flaherty (eds.), *Challenging Times: The Women's Movement in Canada and the United States.* Montreal and Kingston: McGill-Queen's University Press, pp. 120-135.

Howe, F. 1984. *Myths of Coeducation.* Bloomington: Indiana University Press.

Kirst-Ashman, K. K. 1992. "Feminist Values and Social Work: A Model for Educating NonFeminists." *Arete.* 17: 1, 13-25.

Morell, C. 1987. "Cause is Function: Toward a Feminist Model of Integration for Social Work." *Social Service Review.* (March) 61: 1, 144-153.

Pennel, J., Flaherty, M., Gravel, N., Milliken, E. and Neuman, M. 1993. "Feminist Social Work Education in Mainstream and Nonmainstream Classrooms." *AFFILIA* 8 (3): 317-338.

Perlman, H. H. 1989. *Looking Back to See Ahead.* Chicago: Chicago University Press.

Ramsay, R. 1991. "Preparing to Influence Paradigm Shifts in Health Care Strategies," in Taylor, P. and J. Devereux (eds.), *Social Work Administrative Practice in Health Care Settings.* Toronto: Canadian Scholars' Press.

Richard, B. K. 1990. "Feminist Faculty Field Supervision." *Connections.* (March) 3: 8-14.

Specht, H. 1990. "Social Work and the Popular Psychotherapies." *Social Service Review.* (September) 445-457.

Tice, K. 1990. "Gender and Social Work Education: Directions for the 1990's." *Journal of Social Work Education.* 26: 2, 134-144.

Valentich, M. 1986. "Feminism and Social Work Practice," in Turner, Francis J. (ed.), *Social Work Treatment*, 3rd edition. The Free Press: New York, pp. 564-589.

Vinton, L. and Nelson-Gardell, D. 1993. "Consciousness-Raising through Teaching about the Global Oppression of Women." *AFFILIA*. 8: 1, 91-102.

Weick, A. 1987. "Reconstructing the Philosophical Perspective of Social Work." *Social Service Review*. (June) 218-230.

Weick, A., Rapp, C., Sullivan, W. P. and Kisthardt, W=. 1989. "A Strengths Perspective for Social Work Practice." *Social Work*. (July) 350-354.

Wilbur, K. 1981. *No Boundary*. Boston: Shambhala.

Wilbur, K. 1990. *Eye to Eye: The Quest for a New Paradigm*. Boston: Shambhala.

Williams, D. 1992. "The Glass Escalator: Hidden Advantages for Men in the 'Female Professions'." *Social Problems*. 39: 253-265.

Chapter IX
Women's Status, Global Issues and Social Work

Patricia Taylor
Catherine Daly

It is generally accepted that women's status is reflected in the family, the social, legal, political, educational and employment institutions of society. These institutions can promote inequality of equality for women.

One author has suggested that the harmonious functioning of capitalistic patriarchal societies is dependent upon a female subservient class (O'Brien, 1991). Iglitzen and Ross (1976) suggest that in every country, power and responsibility are distributed unequally between men and women. To explain equality and inequality between the sexes, some authors consider that women's inferior status worldwide is the result of systematic discrimination based on sex (Freeman, 1979; Tavris, 1992). Few men are likely to promote women's equality by surrendering power and assuming traditionally feminine responsibilities.

In Canada, the presence of many different cultural perspectives complicates gender inequality. Consequently, conflicts with social work policy and practice often arise. The dilemma for social work education is to prepare students who are able to provide comprehensive services to women of all cultures.

Introduction

The three concepts of feminism, sexism and patriarchy affect all women. The first, feminism, is defined as women suffering from systematic social injustice because of their sex (Richards, 1982). The second, sexism, has two components; men and women are equal but what men do is more important, and women's status is based on a male standard (Freeman, 1979). The third, patriarchy, is a system of male authority that oppresses women through its social, political and economic institutions (Hume, 1989) or a sexual system of power in which the male possesses superior power and economic image (Eisenstein, 1979). These definitions lead to the question: Why should social work teach about women's status from a global perspective? In order to answer this question it is necessary to identify the price of sexism to women worldwide and to identify the sources of women's inequality. Various women's movements have set out to redefine traditional norms for women on a local and global scale, however, gender discrimination continues. Although women's unequal status may no longer be considered right and natural by women or governments, many countries are still patriarchal — promoting a standard for being human based on a male norm (Tavris, 1992; Eisenstein, 1979).

Some statistics highlight the disparity in status between men and women. In 1988, Canadian women constituted 51 per cent of the population. Globally they represent one-half of the world's population (World Development Report, 1989). By virtue of their number alone women possess potential political power. Yet such power has rarely been realized.

Women and Health

In many nations, women are making progress toward greater equality in education, legal status and the right to choose when to have children (Unicef, 1993). Fertility rates are declining in all regions of the developed world. The proportion of the world's married women using contraceptives has risen to an estimated 50 per cent (Unicef, 1993). But one pregnancy in every five is unwanted and unplanned. Approximately one-half million women in the world die in childbirth every year (Unicef, 1993). These statistics do not take into account all the poor women who die of illegal abortions because contraception is unavailable. Similarly, approximately one child in three is malnourished and the most seriously affected are children under the age of five.

Women still outlive men in most societies (Unicef, 1993). Robin Morgan (1984) suggests that since women face such physical challenges as menarche, menstruation, pregnancy, child-bearing, lactation and menopause in addition to the general health problems they share with men, the crisis in world health is a crisis of women.

Similarly, it is often women who are most affected by the destruction of nature. For example, deforestation lowers the water table. Consequently, women, as the world's principal water-haulers and fuel-gatherers, must walk further to find water. Women also lose days and weeks with illnesses resulting from the unsafe water (Unicef, 1993). Other women in developed countries find that toxic waste and polluted water negatively affect their health and that of their families.

Woman and Work

Women constitute the majority of the poor, the underemployed and the economically and socially disadvantaged in most societies in the world today. In Europe and North America, women constitute over 40 per cent of the paid labour force (Morgan, 1984) and contribute more than 46 per cent of the gross domestic product in unpaid labour in the home. In Canada, women's domestic unpaid labour constitutes 46.3 per cent of the GNP (Statistics Canada, 1993). Although women constitute one-third of the workforce worldwide, they still receive less income. On the average their wages are 30 to 40 per cent less than those of men (Unicef, 1993). The majority of women are still paid only one-half to three-quarters the salary that men earn at the same jobs. They are still "ghettosized" into lower paying, "female-intensive" jobs. In Canada, women remain concentrated in traditional fields such as clerical, sales and service. Over 62.2 per cent of social workers in Canada are women but they constituted only .04 per cent of all female workers in 1981 (Armstrong and Armstrong, 1986). Women are responsible for growing most of the world's food, caring for the old and ill, fetching water, cooking, cleaning, washing and shopping (Unicef, 1993).

Furthermore, women suffer from the additional burdens imposed by gender biased hierarchies and subordination. Though under-remunerated and undervalued, women's work is vital to survival in all societies. In many societies, women are the poorest paid and the first to be fired. The sexual division of labour and the secondary status of working women is viewed as natural. "Women's work" is generally considered demeaning to men. It is often accepted as a male prerogative to be personally served by women within the home. For example, worldwide, women work an average of 13 hours a week more than men (Unicef, 1993). In Canada, women who work outside the home do 65.9 per cent of household work (Statistics Canada, 1993). There is much discussion about the problems of the "super mom" and stress. However, the preponderance of evidence contradicts this popular idea. Tavris (1992) notes that women who juggle both family and work are better off although they are more tired. In the role of "super mom" the onus of responsibility remains on individual women enabling societal institutions to avoid the responsibility. The burden of adjustment is on the individual woman.

Women and Violence

Women are controlled by the threat of violence whether it be physical or psychological. The first type restricts physical mobility and the second type limits women's opportunities by restricting norms for women's behaviour. Rape and other forms of sexual abuse are not individual acts. They are assaults against the person (McLaren, 1988). Female circumcision is a form of sexual violence, which has been traditionally practised in some countries to ensure female virginity and honour and to maintain male control of girls and women (Daly, 1978; Saadawi, 1980). In many societies, public spaces are physically dominated by men limiting women's mobility and often their ability to earn a livelihood. For example, in areas where women work shifts, the threat of male violence going to and from work is a constant concern to women. Men are often oblivious to the extent to which fears of sexual aggression control women's lives. Violence against women is a major threat to their equality. For many women, violence begins in the home, and society tends to tolerate violence directed against women. For example, a Spanish riddle reads:

Question: What do mules and women have in common?

Answer: A good beating makes them both better. (United Nations, 1991)

Stereotyping

The theme that crosses all countries is that gender-based subordination is deeply ingrained in the consciousness of both men and women and is usually viewed as a natural corollary of biological differences (Tavris, 1992). Sexual stereotyping is an effective propaganda instrument that serves to maintain the status quo. Sex role stereotyping begins in early childhood (Mackie, 1991). Stereotypes promote the idea that men are normal and women are deficient and they should be more like men to become equal. The dichotomy of male/female roles are deeply ingrained and glorified in language, education, mass media and advertising to the point where many women become desensitized to the extent of their own inferior portrayal. Male-dominated society with male-oriented values and beliefs has existed for so long and is so universal that it has lead to ridicule and insults directed at women, their bodies, mental capacities and social behaviour.

The Law

One of the most significant areas affecting women's status from a global and local perspective is the law. Historically women enjoyed a wide range of legal rights, citizenship, education and political power. Gradually women were stripped of their rights before the law: the right to property and inheritance, to control their bodies, to education and to employment. Despite significant progress in the status of women vis-a-vis the law, equality continues to allude the majority of women (United Nations, 1991). Often women may have equality in the law but inequality continues in practice. This contradiction has an historical basis. The

English jurist Blackstone stated under English Common Law that "the very being or legal existence of the woman is suspended during the marriage or at least is incorporated and consolidated" (Newland, 1989). Traditionally, married women were obligated to surrender control of property to the husband. The education and religion of children were determined by the father, and in the case of divorce, custody was generally awarded to him. The author of the Code of Napoleon stated that "nature intended women to be our slaves. They are our property, we are not theirs. They belong to us just as a tree that bears fruit belongs to a gardener. Women are nothing but machines for producing children" (Newland, 1989). Traditionally, married women were classed with children and "persons of unsound mind" as incapable of entering into contracts. To hold a job or attend a university a woman had first to secure her husband's formal permission. Obedience to her husband was a legal obligation for the married woman. Laws can limit women's aspirations and add to human suffering, or they can provide tools to combat discrimination and promote equality.

The United States Equal Rights Amendment states, "equality of rights under the law shall not be denied or abridged by the United States or by any state on account of sex" (Newland, 1989). Although reflecting a stormy history, the ERA was passed by the Senate in 1972, approved by the House of Representatives and never ratified by the states. Whereas in Canada women's equality is guaranteed by the Charter of Rights and Freedoms.

Legal guarantees of sexual equality are sometimes more cosmetic than real. In many countries a legal guarantee may exist alongside discriminatory legislation. Even if the law provides women equal rights and equal recognition, the social customs of the country may consider the privacy of the home to supersede the law. For example, in Canada and the United States until recently, married women could not testify against their husbands.

Women and Education

In most countries, girls stand a better chance of going to school. However, according to Unicef (1993) 26.5 per cent of the adult world population are illiterate, 19.4 per cent are men, 33.6 per cent are women. In developing countries, over 45 per cent of the women are illiterate. In Canada, approximately 95 per cent of women are literate. There is a direct correlation between women's literacy, health, economic and political power. The nature of women's contributions and the many types of discrimination they suffer represent one of the world's greatest injustices and inefficiencies (Unicef, 1993). Discrimination against women in technology, training and credit reduces the productivity of one-half of the population (Unicef, 1993). Lost opportunities, child health and poverty are related to the status of women. Similarly, male decision-making about family size continues to adversely affect the health of women and children. Empowering women with basic literacy is related to greater uses of social services, the ability to obtain higher income, reduction of child death and reduced family size.

Implications for Social Work Education

Global issues affecting women require local action for two reasons: Canada is a multicultural society and social workers have a commitment to social justice. The *United Way of America* (1987) trends study suggests that the most compelling problem social workers will face in the twenty-first century will be the effect that poverty has on women's lives. Since the majority of the poor in the world will be sole parents with children, the concept of "vulnerable populations" takes on new meaning for social work. Harry Specht (1990) states that social workers should be the conscience of the community. They have a responsibility to create a more sane and humane world, one that enables women to rediscover a sense of meaning, self-worth and control over their lives and their environment. Specht criticizes the traditional social work belief in the individual's potential for change. He believes that most social work educators are taught to think and act in psychotherapeutic terms. They then educate students to follow suit so they also learn to value the psychotherapeutic role. Thus, the vast majority of women social work students want to be clinicians. Specht considers psychiatry, psychoanalysis and psychology inappropriate as the sole means for dealing with social problems and promoting social justice. Since most of the consumers that social workers serve are women, this leads to the idea that individual women are the source of their problems rather than the social context in which they live. When this belief is translated to the educational context, students, who are mostly women, may be seen as being responsible for their individual problems rather than looking for causes within the educational system.

If social work educators want women to value the diversity of women in the world, they have to value the diversity of students. Differences in style and expression should not be confused with differences in the capacity to learn. "Binery thinking," thinking in opposites — male/female, rich/poor, teacher/ student — tends to diminish the dignity and complexity of people's lives, particularly women. Students should be encouraged to question laws, policies and procedures and to assess the effects that these have on the lives of women. Teaching students that there is no therapeutic blueprint for solving women's problems creates an opportunity to redefine the problem itself. Encouraging students to ask the right questions is ultimately the most dynamic approach to social justice.

The social work educator needs to demystify social work as an omnipotent profession by promoting reciprocal learning in the classroom. When this occurs in the classroom it becomes a model for the field. Women in social work education need to stop glorifying "false claims" of objectivity and neutrality as tools of the profession. Finally, if as educators we depersonalize the emotions of students, they in turn will depersonalize their female clients and co-workers. By helping students become more aware of gender issues we seek to eliminate the deleterious effects of prescribed sex roles.

References

Armstrong, P. and Armstrong, H. 1986. "Women's Work in the Labour Force." *The Double Ghetto Canadian Women and Their Segregated Work.* Toronto: McClelland and Stewart.

Daly, M. 1978. *Gyn/Ecology.* Boston: Beacon Press, pp. 109-178.

Eisenstein, Z. 1979. *Capitalist Patriarchy and the Case For Socialist Feminism.* New York: Monthly Review Press.

Freeman, J. 1979. *Women A Feminist Perspective,* 2nd edition. Palo Alto: Mayfield Publishing.

Hume, M. 1989. *The Dilemma of Feminist Theory.* Hamstead England: Harvester Wheat Sheaf Press.

Iglitzen and Ross, R. (eds.). 1976. *Women in the World: Studies in Comparative Patterns.* Santa Barbara: Clio Books.

Mackie, M. (ed.). 1991. *Gender Relations in Canada.* Toronto: Holt, Rinehart and Winston.

McLaren, A. T. (ed.). 1988. "Creating a Canadian Women's Sociology." *Gender and Society.* Toronto: Copp Clark Pitman.

Morgan, R. 1984. *Sisterhood is Global.* Great Britain: Penguin Books.

Newland, K. 1989. *The Sisterhood of Man. The Impact of Women's Changing on Social and Economic Development Around the World.* New York: W. W. Norton.

O'Brien, M. 1991. "The Dialectics of Reproduction," in Mackie, M. (ed.), *Gender Relations in Canada.* Toronto: Holt, Rinehart and Winston, pp. 99-107.

Richards, J. R. 1982. *The Skeptical Feminist: A Philosophical Enquiry.* Harmondsworth: Penguin Books.

Saadawi, E. N. 1980. "The Hidden Face of Eve." *Women in the Arts World,* 2nd edition. London: Zed Press.

Specht, H. 1990. "Social Work and the Popular Psychotherapies." *Social Service Review.* (September) 445-457.

Statistics Canada. 1988. *Women in Canada Statistical Report: Highlights,* p. vii.

Statistics Canada. 1991. *Labour Force Activity of Women by Presence of Children,* pp. 93-325.

Statistics Canada. 1993. *National Income and Expenditure Accounts* (4th quarter).

Statistics Canada. 1993. *Women in the Workplace,* 2nd edition. Target Groups Project.

Tavris, C. 1992. *Mismeasure of Women.* New York: Touchstone Books.

Unicef. 1993. "The Progress of Nations." New York.

United Nations. 1991. "Women's Challengers to the Year 2000." New York.

United Way of America. 1987. "What Lies Ahead Looking Toward the Nineties: A Report." New York.

Women: A World Report. 1985. A New Internationalist Book. London: Methuen.

World Development Report. 1989. Financial Systems and Development: World Development Indicators. Oxford University Press.

World Health Organization. 1992. World Statistics Annual. Geneva.